ABOUT DON HERRON'S
DASHIELL HAMMETT TOUR

"A hard-boiled stroll through the world of the American Private Eye."

— *The New York Times*

" 'Samuel Dashiell Hammett was born May 27, 1894,' Herron begins and for the three hours or so, Hammett and the San Francisco of the 1920s come to life again."

— *San Francisco Chronicle*

"Hardly ever have the city and story been so perfectly matched as are San Francisco and Dashiell Hammett's *The Maltese Falcon* . . . . Hammett shows San Francisco at its most glamourous, dangerous, and intriguing. The City is full of Hammett landmarks, and if you want to see them all take the Dashiell Hammett Tour. . . ."

— *San Francisco Examiner*

"Those of us who have promised ourselves we would map out a walking tour of Hammett's San Francisco have been bested. It's been done! Not only done — but done well, with a loving attention to detail. Don Herron has put this tour together and it's a winner."

— *Mystery*

"The tour started near City Hall. Herron likes to talk and he talked plenty. A traffic light said walk. Herron walked. The group moved like a drunken cat through the streets and back alleys of the Tenderloin. It passed Southeast Asian diners, tawdry hotels, bars without windows, and places where a twenty will buy you more than the weekend's groceries. Herron moved fast. The group wheezed up Nob Hill, then down, into Burritt where Miles Archer bought it. It wasn't a pretty place. . . ."

— *Wall Street Journal*

THE
DASHIELL HAMMETT
TOUR
by
Don Herron

CITY LIGHTS BOOKS
San Francisco

Cover design by John Miller, Big Fish Books
Cover photograph, courtesy of Bettmann Archives
Maps by Don Herron

Photo credits:

California Historical Society. p: 96
Claire Fairbanks Cross. p: 44
Don Herron collection. pp: 12, 23, 32, 43
Frontispiece. Courtesy of John's Grill.
William Kostura. pp: 84, 88, 91, 98, 116, and photographic copies of
    archival materials
San Francisco Archives, San Francisco Public Library. pp: 105, 118, 124
Mary Spoerer. pp: 53, 58, 65, 70, 79, 82, 89, 92, 93, 99, 109, 114, 127

Library of Congress Cataloging-in-Publication Data
Herron, Don.
    The Dashiell Hammett tour : a guidebook / by Don Herron.
        p.   cm.
    ISBN 0-87286-264-X : $9.95
    1. Hammett, Dashiell, 1894–1961 — Homes and haunts — California
    — San Francisco — Guide-books.   2. Literary landmarks —
    California — San Francisco — Guide-books.   3. San Francisco
    (Calif.) — Description — Guide-books.   I. Title.
    PS3515.A4347Z692   1991
    813'.52 — dc20
    [B]   91-21314
                                                                    CIP

City Lights Books are available to bookstores through our primary
distributor: Subterranean Company, P. O. Box 168, 265 S. 5th St.,
Monroe, OR 97456. Our Books are also available through library
jobbers and regional distributors. For personal orders and catalogs,
please write to City Lights Books, 261 Columbus Avenue, San
Francisco, CA 94133.

CITY LIGHTS BOOKS are edited by Lawrence Ferlinghetti and
Nancy J. Peters and published at the City Lights Bookstore,
261 Columbus Avenue, San Francisco, CA 94133.

for Brigid & Nick

CONTENTS

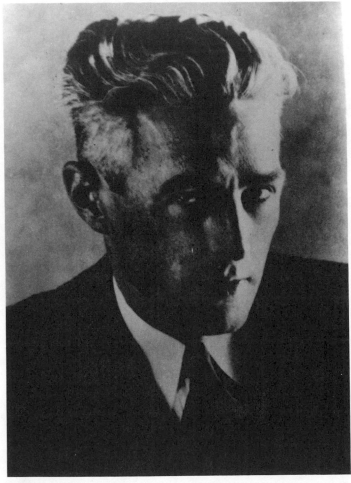

Dashiell Hammett, 1920s

DASHIELL HAMMETT

Samuel Dashiell Hammett was born May 27, 1894, in St. Mary's County, Maryland, and died January 10, 1961, in the city of New York. In those sixty-six years he became a revolutionary force in popular fiction in this country, the seminal twentieth-century mystery writer, pioneering an authentic American style for the tale of crime and murder. And it was while living in San Francisco that Hammett reinvented the form, creating in a series of furnished rooms from the Tenderloin to Nob Hill the modern hard-boiled detective story.

Hammett came to San Francisco in summer, 1921. Before he left in the fall of 1929, he had written most of his fiction, including the landmark novels *Red Harvest* and *The Maltese Falcon*, as well as *The Big Knockover*, *The Dain Curse*, and the beginning of *The Glass Key*. All but two handfuls of his more than one hundred short stories were created in his apartments on Eddy, Turk, Hyde, Post, and Leavenworth Streets. More than half his fiction takes place in The City. His characters Sam Spade — blond, slope-shouldered, Satan-faced — and the Continental Op — a nameless short fat detective — gumshoed grooves in the foggy streets of Frisco. And Nick and Nora Charles, visiting in New York when the thin man is murdered, were also residents here.

Hammett's San Francisco stands as one of the great literary treatments of a city; it has been compared with Joyce's Dublin and Dickens' London for its evocation of time and place — 1920s San Francisco when night-fog cloaked the hills and a host of sinister customers were afoot. In the Continental Op tales the unnamed operative for the Continental Detective Agency goes into every neighborhood and encounters every level of society, from bankers with wandering daughters in Pacific Heights mansions to cheap gunmen living in barren rooms in Tenderloin hotels, who do their drinking in North Beach speakeasies.

In *The Maltese Falcon* Hammett created a plot as glamourous as San Francisco itself, adding new luster and legend to The City. Sam Spade in snap-brim hat and trenchcoat, stalking through the fog, is as firm a part of San Francisco's lore as the 1906 earthquake and fire are of her history. No other novel has excited so much interest here, or sent so many people scurrying over the hills to shadow Spade's movements in his search for the fabulous figurine of a mysterious black bird.

•

Born into a working class family, the son of Richard Thomas Hammett and Annie Bond Dashiell, Hammett was raised with his sister and brother in the cities of Philadelphia and Baltimore. Frequently down on their luck, they lived in Baltimore for several years off and on in 212 North Stricker Street, a house rented by Hammett's maternal grandmother. Whenever they got more money, they would rent a separate apartment for themselves, but invariably they came back to North Stricker.

When Hammett was fourteen, his father became too sick to work. It was expected, and it was necessary, that Hammett as the oldest son would quit Baltimore Polytechnic Institute, the high school where he had enrolled, to get a job and help support the family until his father became well enough to take up the slack as the major breadwinner. Once he went to work, Hammett did not go back to high school. He would never attend college.

From the apartments and flats the family lived in, Hammett held down a long series of short-lived jobs through the remainder of his teenage years. Initially he worked for the Baltimore and Ohio Railroad. In time he served as a stevedore, messenger, and freight clerk. For a while he operated a nail machine in a box factory. These jobs bored him, and often he did not show up for work on time. As he later wrote in a letter to *Black Mask*, the mystery magazine where most of his fiction first saw print, "after a fraction of a year in high school . . . I became the unsatisfactory and unsatisfied employee of various railroads, stock brokers, machine manufacturers, canners, and the like. Usually I was fired."

Nineteen-fifteen was the year, Hammett recalled, that he began what became the cornerstone job on which he built his career as a writer. He was twenty-one years old, and once again out of work. Looking through the job ads in the Baltimore paper, he came to an oddly-worded but intriguing notice. From the manner in which the ad was worded, he could not tell what kind of job it offered. Speaking of it later, he suggested that the ad had a sense of glamour or adventure to it — perhaps something like the sense of danger the Pony Express ads of the nineteenth century imparted when they calmly stated, "Orphans Preferred."

Hammett decided to give it a shot. The employment ad took him to the Continental Building in downtown Baltimore. The new job: hire in as an operative for the Pinkerton National Detective Agency.

●

The Pinkerton agency was started in 1850 in Chicago by the Scots immigrant Allan Pinkerton. During the Civil War, Union President Abraham Lincoln gave Pinkerton and his operatives the assignment to spy on the Confederacy. With Union victory, Pinkerton consolidated his position, building a business that became, in effect, the largest nationwide law enforcement agency until J. Edgar Hoover began his reign in 1924 over what would become the Federal Bureau of Investigation. Newspaper accounts of Hoover's G-Men in pursuit of John Dillinger or Machine Gun Kelly during the Depression are like echoes of Pinkerton's operatives hounding Jesse and Frank James and the Younger Brothers in the years following the War Between the States. At the time Hammett hired in, Allan Pinkerton's son William was still in charge of the organization.

Over the next seven years, Hammett traveled America as a Pinkerton man. The job introduced him to a wide variety of people, places, and types of crime. In the early days of World War I, Hammett said he was assigned to shadow a man around Washington, D.C. who was suspected of being a German spy. He wrote that the man was not a secret agent for Germany, but he *was* the single most boring suspect he ever had to trail during his detective career — and added that he used this man as the model for Caspar Gutman, the fat man in *The Maltese Falcon*. In Pasco, Washington, he nabbed an oily little guy who had been forging checks. This fellow served as the model for the perfumed rogue Joel Cairo in the Sam Spade novel. Spade's secretary Effie Perrine was based on a woman, Hammett wrote, who "once asked me to go into the narcotic smuggling business with her in San Diego."

In Stockton, California, working out of the San Francisco office, Hammett was assigned to look for a man who had smashed in the window of a jewelry store in San Jose and boosted the display jewels. He could not find that guy. He did, however, put the arm on a criminal he said the Stockton papers had labeled the Midget Bandit. A week earlier, the Midget Bandit had stuckup a filling station in Stockton, then fled to Los Angeles. The owner of the station, interviewed by the press, chose to make some unfortunate remarks about the robber. He described the Midget Bandit as "a runt" and suggested what he might do if the runt ever showed his face again. These remarks turned out to be unwise — apparently the Midget Bandit collected his press clippings. He bought the Stockton papers to read the daring account of his robbery, saw the comments on his size, stole a car and drove back to Stockton to see what the owner *would* do the second time, with a gun held down on him. Hammett recognized him as "a fair pick-up," put the arm on him, and turned him over to the police. When he came to write *The Maltese Falcon*, he used the Midget Bandit as the model for Wilmer Cook, the young gunman traveling with Gutman, who threatens to "fog" Sam Spade if he doesn't "lay off."

In New York in the 1940s, over lunch in Luchow's Restaurant, Hammett told Frederic Dannay (who wrote, in collaboration with his cousin Manfred B. Lee, under the name "Ellery Queen"), that the Continental Op was modeled on Pinkerton Assistant Superintendent James Wright of the Baltimore office. Jimmy Wright, he stated, gave him his initial training. Since the Continental Detective Agency in his stories is modeled directly on Pinkerton, it now is taken as a given that the name for the fictitious agency derives from the Continental Building in Baltimore where Hammett first took instruction in detection from Wright.

Hammett claimed he got his first promotion with Pinkerton by capturing a man who had stolen a Ferris wheel. Tantalizingly, that was usually all he said about it. When he went into more detail, he said the episode occurred when he was working in Idaho and Montana. To find the stolen Ferris wheel, he went around to every carnival in the area until he found one of the machines without a proper bill of sale. Mystery solved. But then he mentioned that after he had turned the thief and the Ferris wheel over to the local police, the man proceeded to escape, *taking the Ferris wheel with him*. He was never caught again.

Good reason exists to doubt some of Hammett's accounts of his Pinkerton exploits. As early as 1923 in letters to *Black Mask* and in an article for *Smart Set* called "From the Memoirs of a Private Detective," Hammett began to parlay his years as a sleuth into a glamourous-sounding background, from which his fiction leapt, alive with realistic detail, onto the page. Still, while it is possible to imagine a stolen Ferris wheel, it is a big strain to imagine a *jailbreak* with a stolen Ferris wheel.

One fact remains clear: whether the incidents related by Hammett are complete lies, only partial fabrications, or in other cases the actual truth about what happened during his days as a detective, this line of work was infinitely more interesting than operating a nail machine in a box factory outside Baltimore.

●

Some aspects of detective work could not be made to sound glamourous — consequently, Hammett did not refer to them directly in statements made for print, and seems to have refrained from talking about them much among his friends. By the time he began working for the agency, Pinkerton dealt far less with robberies, kidnappings, and murders than one might expect after scanning "From the Memoirs of a Private Detective." More and more of their income, and that of every other large detective agency in America, came from acting as strikebreakers against the unions organizing across the country. The largest purchaser of the Thompson submachine gun was not the growing ranks of gangsterdom, but the Pinkerton National Detective Agency, with pro-union forces coming face-to-face with rows of Pinks at the factory gates, tommy guns held ready. Working for Pinkerton in that era, Hammett undoubtedly did a lot of strikebreaking.

In fact, Hammett probably began as a strikebreaker with Pinkerton rather than as an investigator, based upon his description of the employment ad he answered, one that did not tell exactly what kind of job he was applying for, but made it sound interesting and exciting. Leo Huberman in *The Labor Spy Racket* (1937) described the manner in which detective agencies would "hook" factory workers, offering them extra money if they wrote daily reports on unionizing activities. Using information uncovered by the Subcommittee of the Committee on Education and Labor hearings conducted by Senator Bob La Follette, Huberman goes into detail on how the agencies groomed their stoolpigeons and union-busters, and notes:

> But sometimes the plant setup is such that
> an outside operative can be brought in without
> causing undue suspicion. The agencies
> usually recruit these outside operatives by the
> "blind ad" method.... They look like any

> other ad. But they are not.... Any applicant
> who writes an intelligent reply to a blind ad is
> notified to call for an interview at a stated
> address. The name on the door may be the
> John Smith Company or Green Engineering
> Corporation or any other name — except the
> name of the detective agency.... If the
> interviewer is satisfied that he is capable, he is
> told that a job will be found for him at such
> and such a factory; he will receive his wages
> for his work at the factory, and an additional
> sum for the daily reports he is to write. The
> applicant next applies at the factory, is given
> the job at once, and his career as a stoolpigeon
> is begun.

Given his commonplace work experience up to 1915, it is
easy to picture Hammett pulled into Pinkerton employ in
yet another factory by the blind ad method. From that
point, it also is easy to see his intelligence being
recognized, and soon utilized, as his supervisor decided to
move him up to full operative status, which resulted in
many more strikebreaking assignments. For the irony
involved, it is worth noting that Leo Huberman would be
one of the people Hammett's good friend Lillian Hellman
appealed to in 1951, when she was trying to raise bail
money for Hammett as the juggernaut forces backed by
Senator Joseph McCarthy and HUAC were preparing to
send him to prison. Huberman and some others offered to
put up the money to aid the ex-strikebreaker. Bail was
denied.

In her book *Scoundrel Time* (1976), about those years
dominated by the House Committee on UnAmerican
Activities, Lillian Hellman suggests that Hammett's later
communist political philosophy was an eventual reaction
to the experiences he had as a strikebreaker — and the
realization that he had been working on the wrong side.
Specifically, he told her that he worked as a Pinkerton
strikebreaker in 1917 for the Anaconda Copper Company
in Butte, Montana, against the Industrial Workers of the
World, the Wobblies. He told his family about this period,
too; his oldest daughter, Mary Jane, is quoted as having
asked him: " 'You mean you were working for Pinkerton
against the IWW?' And he said, 'That's right.' " His

daughter added, "He told me he was not politically aware at that time.... He was strictly out to do his job."

During their first months together in 1930, Hellman says Hammett told her about the Butte job, about how an officer of the Anaconda Copper Company had offered him five thousand dollars to assassinate the labor organizer Frank Little, in town at that time rallying the copper miners. She said the realization that he had been a strikebreaker made her think, *I don't want to be with this man*. When she told him that, he said, "Yes, ma'am, why do you think I told you?" Hellman said, "He seldom talked about the past unless I asked questions, but through the years he was to repeat that bribe offer so many times that I came to believe ... that it was a kind of key to his life. He had given a man the right to think he would murder, and the fact that Frank Little was lynched ... must have been, for Hammett, an abiding horror. I think I can date Hammett's belief that he was living in a corrupt society from Little's murder. In time, he came to the conclusion that nothing less than a revolution could wipe out the corruption. I do not mean to suggest that his radical conversion was based on one experience, but sometimes in complex minds it is the plainest experience that speeds the wheels that have already begun to move."

Hammett said he turned down the offer. Five thousand dollars in 1917 was a tremendous amount of money — he was making under one hundred dollars a month with Pinkerton. Six other men had less scruples. Little, a one-eyed, half-Indian labor organizer, by that time on the IWW General Executive Board, spoke at a miners' meeting on July 31st. About 3 a.m. on August 1st he was dragged from his room by six armed and masked men. One of Little's legs was still in a cast from an earlier brush with vigilantes. The men roped him to the back of a car and dragged him to the outskirts of Butte. According to Wobbly accounts, the men castrated Frank Little before lynching him from a railroad trestle. The note pinned to his swaying body read: "First and last warning 3-7-77" — 3-7-77 being an old vigilante warning symbol, purportedly based on the dimensions of a grave. The note was initialed six times, with the initials matching the first names of six union officials in Butte.

In his biography of Hammett, *Shadow Man* (1981), Richard Layman states that the story of "Hammett's peripheral involvement" in the murder of Frank Little "is implausible." In 1982, however, the Butte bookstore owner Richard Green developed a theory that not only was Hammett involved, he had *not* turned down the offer. Green cites Hellman's statement regarding the offer. Then he notes that in his 1921 novel *100 Percent*, the radical writer Upton Sinclair fictionalized the lynching of an IWW organizer in which a character named Hammett participated. Green's most tempting piece of evidence is the description of the lynch party given by Little's landlady, in which one of the men is said to be about five foot eleven, thin, maybe twenty years old. Hammett stood about six foot one, was thin throughout his life, and in August 1917 was twenty-three years old. Whether or not Hammett was involved is unknown, since Frank Little's murder has never been solved, officially. But no doubt exists that Hammett did work as a strikebreaker or that he was familiar with Butte.

Hammett's vision of a hard-boiled universe for his fiction clearly derives from his direct participation as a Pinkerton op in the war raging between labor and management during the 'teens. His first hardcover novel, *Red Harvest* (1929), is set in a city named Personville, nicknamed "Poisonville," and completely recognizable as Butte. André Gide later called *Red Harvest* "the last word in atrocity, cynicism, and horror," yet many other critics naively have assumed that the landslide of violence portrayed in the book — thirty-odd deaths courtesy of dynamiting, machine guns, pistols, knives, and ice-picks — was greatly exaggerated. They do not take into account the tremendous violence of the time. On October 30, 1916, forty Wobblies came to Everett, Washington, to protest the arrest of IWW agitators. They were clubbed and taken to jail. That night the Wobblies were taken out, stripped, and forced to run a gauntlet of several hundred vigilantes who beat the naked men with guns, clubs, and whips. Wobblies called this night the Everett Massacre, but it hardly ranks with the *Red Harvest*-like scenario of November 5th, when two hundred and fifty Wobblies chartered a boat up Puget Sound to demonstrate against the "massacre." Alerted by private detectives, sheriff's deputies met the boat at the dock. Someone — which side unknown — fired a first shot. By the time the boat cast loose and fled from the gunfire, four men aboard were dead, another was dying, and thirty-one were wounded. Several had fallen overboard and were never recovered. On the dock, one deputy was dead, another would die, and twenty-one were wounded.

•

During World War I Hammett interrupted work with Pinkerton, enlisting in the Motor Ambulance Corps in June, 1918. His year of service was spent about thirty miles from Baltimore; he did not go overseas or get near actual combat. Most of his time was spent in the army hospital. In 1918 an epidemic of Spanish influenza swept the world, killing hundreds of thousands of people in America alone. Hammett was one of the lucky ones who lived through the sickness, but while he was hospitalized with the flu he went on to develop tuberculosis, which would plague his health off and on for many years.

By May, 1919, Hammett was out of the service and well enough to go back into detective work. In 1920 he transferred to the Pinkerton office in Spokane, Washington. Suddenly the tuberculosis again became active. That November he found himself a patient in a U.S. Public Health Service hospital located on the Puyallup Road, which ran between Tacoma and Seattle. The place had been an Indian school for the Puyallup tribe until converted into hospital use at the end of World War I. According to Hammett, the patients were half "lungers," half victims of shellshock. Here at the Cushman Hospital Hammett met a pretty young nurse named Josephine Dolan.

Later she said that Hammett was quiet, well-dressed, and would read to the other patients. She recalled that they went out to restaurants in downtown Tacoma and on ferryboat rides. The romance was disrupted when Hammett was moved to Camp Kearny, near San Diego, and she was transferred to the Cheyenne Hospital in

Helena, Montana. They kept in touch by mail.

Hammett left Camp Kearny about May, 1921, and returned briefly to Spokane. He spent another week or two in Seattle, then arranged to meet Josephine Dolan in San Francisco, where Pinkerton had assigned him to work as a strikebreaker on the docks for the businessman Blackjack Jerome. Hammett said that Jerome continued the longtime San Francisco tradition of shanghaiing. He would drive a truck through the city in the early hours and round up drunks, then, barreling through the picket lines, he'd have the slowly sobering men at his mercy — they'd give a full day's work, or cross the picket lines alone.

On July 6, 1921, Hammett and Josephine Dolan took out a marriage license. They married July 7th in St. Mary's Cathedral on Van Ness Avenue. Originally they were planning to return to Baltimore and set up housekeeping near Hammett's family, after the job for Blackjack Jerome was finished, but once Hammett had a taste of life in San Francisco, Baltimore seemed considerably less attractive.

Hammett decided to stay in San Francisco. For the first few months, he continued to work for Pinkerton, then, late in 1921 or perhaps early in 1922, he quit. The tuberculosis was flaring up once more, and his health no longer permitted him to do the work. How could he spend hours on his feet shadowing someone, or act tough as a strikebreaker, when with the TB active he had to line up kitchen chairs between the bed and the bathroom, so he could prop himself up to get to the sink to hemorrhage? He needed an easy job, maybe a job he could do at home.

Hammett decided to become a writer. In 1922, funded by the Veterans' Bureau, he enrolled in Munson's Business College on Mission Street, a vocational school where he studied stenography and writing. He stayed with these classes for over a year, by which time he had begun to sell stories to magazines.

With his background as a detective, he quickly saw the likelihood of cracking the detective pulp fiction market. Most of the writers had no idea of what real detective work was about, and their artificial stories proved it. Surely, with his experience he could do just as well —

Looking Down Market Street

View from Twin Peaks

Continential Op Country
Two views of Dashiell Hammett's San Francisco, 1923

and maybe better — with a crime story, and bring in some extra money.

●

Hammett's career as a Pinkerton operative obscured for many people the full scope of his literary ambitions. In the essay "The Simple Art of Murder" (1944), Raymond Chandler, Hammett's major successor in the hard-boiled genre, speculated that Hammett had accomplished his fiction almost by accident — a high school dropout, a job as a detective, a huge native talent, these factors combined to produce a major primitive artist, who wrote what he wrote because it came naturally, not because he was going about it intellectually or perhaps even artistically.

In fact, Hammett seems to have begun writing, as did Chandler, in hopes of becoming a poet, with the fame and respect that is sometimes a poet's due. Beaten down by tuberculosis, Hammett faced his own mortality, and discovered an anomalous craving for some kind of immortality. A lapsed Catholic, religion was not going to serve him to this end. His marriage and start of his own family reflects the need to perpetuate his name, but as the son of an anonymous working class father and grandfathers, he knew having a family would not be enough. Feeling he had a talent for writing, Hammett set his eye on poetry.

Some of the biographers feel Hammett took the classes in the Munson vocational school with plans to become a journalist, which seems unlikely — a reporter in those days held down a schedule not far removed from that of a detective. Hammett surely was smart enough to know he was not going to make enough money to live on from poetry, but might be able to survive by selling squibs and stories to magazines on the side. If he could type fast enough and write clearly enough.

His first publication, a short-short called "The Parthian Shot," appeared in *The Smart Set* for October 1922, under the name Dashiell Hammett. In the December 1922 issues of *Brief Stories* and *Black Mask*, his first crime stories saw print, but under the pen name "Peter Collinson" (slang for "nobody's son") since Hammett appears to have made the decision to save his own name for the publication of his poetry. Ultimately Hammett would satirize his first literary goals in the figure of the sonnet-writing sleuth Robin Thin in the stories "The Nails in Mr. Cayterer" (1926) and the posthumously published "A Man Called Thin" (1962). Working for his father's detective agency in San Francisco, Thin would much prefer to be left alone to write his verse.

With the "Peter Collinson" tales for *Black Mask*, Hammett found a ready market in an area where he had no shortage of ideas. Within a year of his first sale to *The Smart Set*, he dropped the "Peter Collinson" byline. The October 15, 1923 issue of *Black Mask* features, as a matter of fact, *two* Continental Op tales: "Slippery Fingers" appears under the "Collinson" name, and "Crooked Souls" under the name Dashiell Hammett. By 1924 even the short-shorts for *The Smart Set* had been abandoned, as Hammett devoted all his attention to knocking out tales for *Black Mask*.

Hammett was not the first American mystery writer with real experience behind him in detection, and life on the streets. That claim could be put forth for Josiah Flynt, who wandered the country as a hobo and claimed to have served in the late 1800s on the Chicago police force; Flynt's books include *Notes of an Itinerant Policeman* (1900) and *The Rise of Ruderick Clowd* (1903). But Hammett certainly had a far greater talent than Flynt, and more importantly, soon came to an awareness of the literary possibilities of the crime story. His decision to use his own name with the tales for *Black Mask* indicates he knew these stories were a way to make his name known, to achieve some kind of immortality.

Writing in 1944, Raymond Chandler did not have access to letters that are available today, which indicate Hammett's ambitions. The clearest statement of his goals appears in 1928 in a letter to Blanche Knopf, the year before her husband Alfred A. Knopf brought Hammett into hardcover with *Red Harvest*. Dated March 20th of that year, this letter says:

> I'm one of the few — if there are any more — people moderately literate who take the detective story seriously. I don't mean that I

necessarily take my own or anybody else's
seriously — but the detective story as a form.
Some day somebody's going to make
"literature" of it ..., and I'm selfish enough to
have my hopes, however slight the evident
justification may be. I have a long speech I
usually make on the subject, all about the
ground not having been scratched yet, and so
on, but I won't bore you with it now.

Self-educated out of the free and lending libraries of
America, Hammett was an intelligent and voracious
reader with wide-ranging tastes. In the letter to Blanche
Knopf he noted that Ford Madox Ford's *The Good
Soldier* "wouldn't have needed much altering to have
been a detective story." In the Continental Op tale "Fly
Paper" (1929) a woman borrows a method of building
gradual immunity against arsenic from *The Count of
Monte Cristo*, in order to murder her criminal
boyfriend. In the novel *The Dain Curse* (1929) the Op
says, "I had a wisecrack on my tongue — something
about Cabell being a romanticist in the same sense that
the wooden horse was Trojan." And Hammett was
acquainted with far more obscure writers than James
Branch Cabell — in another Op tale, "The Gutting of
Couffignal," (1925) the nameless short fat detective is
found reading *The Lord of the Sea* by M. P. Shiel before
the lights go out and guns start blazing. The Op
provides a capsule review:

The book was called *The Lord of the Sea*,
and had to do with a strong, tough and violent
fellow named Hogarth, whose modest plan
was to hold the world in one hand. There were
plots and counterplots, kidnappings, murders,
prison-breakings, forgeries and burglaries,
diamonds as large as hats and floating forts
larger than Couffignal. It sounds dizzy here,
but in the book it was as real as a dime.

Shiel's speculative novel first appeared in 1901, and
today is considered a science-fiction classic in which the
mulatto author predicts, decades before the founding of
Israel, the creation of a Zionist state, and provides a one-
stop example of the strange literary byways with which
Hammett was familiar.

In an introduction to a Modern Library reprint of *The Maltese Falcon* in 1934, Hammett wrote that the idea for jewel-encrusted statue came about because "somewhere I had read of the peculiar rental agreement between Charles V and the Order of the Hospital of St. John of Jerusalem." Another time he mentioned that *The Maltese Falcon* derived from the Henry James novel *The Wings of the Dove*, perhaps from the way in which Henry James described the allure his heroine had for the other characters, who are "entangled and coerced... drawn in as by some pool of a Lorelei ... inheriting from their connection with her strange difficulties and still stranger opportunities."

●

Today it is fashionable to downgrade Hammett's shorter fiction in favor of the novels. Hammett by the 1930s personally dismissed the shorts and novelettes for *Black Mask*, and wanted his reputation to be assessed by the five novels Alfred A. Knopf published in hardcover: *Red Harvest* (1929), *The Dain Curse* (1929), *The Maltese Falcon* (1930), *The Glass Key* (1931) and *The Thin Man* (1934). In her biography *Dashiell Hammett: A Life* (1983), Diane Johnson quotes from letters Hammett wrote to his wife in which he says he is "Blackmasking" and working "on the *Black Mask* junk," comments which possibly reflect his sardonic and often self-deprecating humor as much as a growing discontent with the pulp magazine marketplace. During his years in San Francisco, Hammett even briefly abandoned crime writing in favor of doing advertising copy for Samuels Jewelers, but then came back to *Black Mask* to produce the novel-length works on which he felt his fame would be based.

The fact is that with the short stories he wrote in San Francisco, Hammett completely revolutionized the way writers in America perceived the mystery story. In 1926, when a new editor named Joseph T. Shaw assumed command of *Black Mask*, he looked over the stories that the magazine had published since its inception in 1920, and recognized Hammett as the standout writer. By that date *Black Mask* already was considered the most prestigious pulp magazine for a mystery writer to appear in, the locus of a new and exciting kind of crime story. As the front quote for his history of the magazine entitled *The Black Mask Boys* (1985), William F. Nolan chose this statement by Russell B. Nye from *The Unembarrassed Muse: The Popular Arts in America*: "The greatest change in the detective story since Poe came in 1926 with the emergence of *Black Mask* school of fiction."

Edgar Allan Poe, of course, created the mystery story as we know it today in the early 1840s, and in only four tales — "Murders in the Rue Morgue," "The Purloined Letter," "The Mystery of Marie Roget," and "The Man in the Box." In these stories Poe came up with the idea of the brilliant amateur detective, who solves puzzles that baffle the official police force, in the person of C. Auguste Dupin of Paris — model for Sherlock Holmes and hundreds more to follow. Dupin's cases are narrated by an admiring friend — origin of Dr. John Watson and a host of similar sidekicks. In only four tales Poe also came up with almost every technical device used in mysteries since then: the locked room puzzle, the least-likely suspect, the mystery based on an actual murder case, et cetera. Until Hammett sat down at the typewriter in Eddy Street, no essential change had been made in the mystery story since Poe had Dupin explain his methods of ratiocination.

In "The Simple Art of Murder" Raymond Chandler made the classic case for the hard-boiled school of detective fiction that came out of *Black Mask*, and said that Dashiell Hammett was "the ace performer." Chandler wrote, "Hammett gave murder back to the kind of people that commit it for a reason, not just to provide a corpse." He said that Hammett wrote "for people with a sharp, aggressive attitude to life. They were not afraid of the seamy side of things; they lived there. Violence did not dismay them; it was right down their street." In a word, Hammett was the first writer to make the crime story realistic, and he did it in the first handful of tales he wrote for *Black Mask*.

As soon as Joseph Shaw began editing *Black Mask*, Hammett became the most influential writer of crime fiction in America since Poe, because Shaw developed one standard: you want to write for my magazine, then write like Dashiell Hammett. (When Raymond Chandler began writing his first mystery stories in the 1930s, Shaw, no fool, loosened up his standard somewhat: okay, now you can write like either Hammett or this new guy Chandler.)

From his first sale to *Black Mask* — "The Road Home" — only his second published story, the essential elements of Hammett's writing that would revolutionize the mystery are evident: a terse, rapid-fire style, as economical as the reports that Hammett had turned in as a Pinkerton operative; as hero, a professional detective; and an offer that tempts the hero to the wrong side of the law. The fugitive in "The Road Home" suggests a partnership in a fabulous bed of gems in exchange for freedom, an offer that preceded by seven years Caspar Gutman's negotiations with Sam Spade over the statue of a jewel-encrusted falcon. The manhunter, Hagedorn, cries: "after all I've gone through you don't expect me to throw them down now — now that the job's as good as done!" When his prey suddenly escapes into the jungle, Hagedorn takes after him, with the doubt raised in the reader's mind — will he bring the criminal to justice, or cash in on his offer? Hammett does not say.

This stark etching of a lawman riding the edge of morality and the law would become a commonplace in *Black Mask*, which became a pulp-paper mirror of a society corrupt on all levels, from the hoodlum on the street to the graft-taking politician in City Hall. Only the detective, alone, is seen as a largely honest man, trying to do his job and stay largely honest.

In the December 1922 issue of *Black Mask* with Hammett's first tale, Carroll John Daly also appeared for the first time with "The False Burton Combs." In May 1923, Daly would be the first writer for the *Mask* to introduce a wise-cracking tough guy detective in "Three Gun Terry," the premiere tale about Terry Mack. Hammett's Continental Op would not appear until October of 1923. While there is no question that Daly established some of the ground rules for the hard-boiled fiction to follow, some commentators have overestimated his importance, suggesting that he beat out Hammett. In fact, they came out of the gate at the same moment, with similar ideas, but in the race to follow, Hammett led the way for writers such as Chandler (whose poetic voice for Philip Marlowe completely eclipsed Daly's blunt narration). Daly, with his simplistic mayhem — the detective fires both pistols at once, yet only *one hole* appears in the forehead of the guy he has just drilled (a swell shot) — led the lesser talents to a deadend in the character of Mike Hammer, whose creator, Mickey Spillane, was a big fan of Daly's writing.

And during the 1920s when Hammett, settled in San Francisco, was working on his initial stories, Ernest Hemingway was in Paris writing *his* first terse tales of violence. The "tough guy" school, a new movement in American letters, as modern as jazz, was springing up spontaneously in the wake of the World War. By the end of the Depression, the hard-boiled story was entrenched in far more venues than *Black Mask*.

●

Even as Hammett began writing the novels in the late twenties that would take his name to national and international fame, his marriage was hitting the skids. When he left San Francisco for New York in fall 1929, he and Josephine Dolan Hammett had separated. From The City she took the two daughters from their marriage to southern California, in expectation that Hammett would be able to see them when he got to Hollywood to write movies.

His ambitions were skyrocketing. Knopf in 1929 issued both *Red Harvest* and *The Dain Curse* in hardcover. Before Hammett left San Francisco he finished a rewrite of the *Black Mask* version of *The Maltese Falcon* for Knopf's 1930 schedule. *The Glass Key* was completed after hitting New York in what Hammett said was a whirlwind of typing, the last third of the novel composed in something like one thirty-hour session. And in 1930 Paramount released the first film based on Hammett's work, *Roadhouse Nights*, credited as coming from both *Red Harvest* and a story by Ben Hecht entitled "The River Inn." *Roadhouse Nights* is the film that introduced Jimmy Durante and his famous nose to the screen, and bears no remarkable resemblance to Hammett's novel.

The Glass Key appeared in four parts in *Black Mask* in 1930, along with two final short stories featuring the Continental Op. After that, *Black Mask* would never again be able to afford the word rates Hammett's fiction could command. From his rooms in 133 East 38th Street in New York, Hammett briefly took up mystery reviewing for the *New York Evening Post*, which he continued after moving to Hollywood later in the year. From 1927 through 1929 Hammett had provided occasional mystery reviews for *The Saturday Review of Literature*, with his first review now seen as the announcement of his intention to sweep all competition away — he trashed *The Benson Murder Case* by "S. S. Van Dine," pen name for Willard Huntington Wright, the bestselling and most respected author of mystery books in America in the twenties. As soon as *Red Harvest* appeared, serious readers abandoned Wright's unlikely plots in favor of the new writer on the scene. The *Post* reviews reinforced Hammett's presence as the hot new mystery writer, but soon he found he did not have time for them. His last reviews for October 1930 were written in 1551 ½ North Bronson Avenue in Hollywood, and quickly Hammett's preferred stopping place became the Beverly Wilshire.

In Hollywood during the winter of 1930 Hammett met Lillian Hellman. She was then the twenty-four year old wife of screenwriter Arthur Kober, apparently an agreeable fellow who made little objection to her going over to live with Hammett. In 1934 the Kobers got a divorce, in the fifth year of the on-and-off relationship with Hellman, which lasted until Hammett's death.

By 1931 it may have seemed to Hammett that he had it made. His original story for the screen, "After School," was released by Paramount, after rewrites by others, as *City Streets*, starring Gary Cooper and Sylvia Sidney. Warner Brothers bought all movie rights to his novel *The Maltese Falcon* for $8,500, producing a movie by that title which today is virtually unknown — *The Maltese Falcon*, directed by Roy Del Ruth, with Ricardo Cortez in the role of Sam Spade and Bebe Daniels as the femme fatale. In all likelihood Hammett may have polished dialogue in other films during his first couple of years in Hollywood. If so, he would have been very well paid and yet have received no screen credit. In this period it is said that he was hired to develop a screen treatment for Greta Garbo as well, which was never produced.

That year Knopf published *The Glass Key* in book form, which Hammett in later years figured to be his best novel. The protagonist is the antihero Ned Beaumont (always called Ned Beaumont, both names, never by one or the other in the clipped reportorial narrative), who works in a sometimes illegal capacity for the crime boss Paul Madvig. The novel explores their relationship and final split against a background of political corruption in an Eastern city, which may be modeled on Baltimore, or perhaps Philadelphia. Here Hammett moves away from the violent carnage of *Red Harvest*, or even the murders of *The Maltese Falcon*, to a subtle but insidious portrayal of psychological threats, including a scene where Ned Beaumont sets up a man so that he commits suicide, and another sequence — quite famous as one of the most brutal ever written — in which Ned Beaumont is held prisoner by some of Madvig's rivals and is systematically beaten by a thug in a sadomasochistic ritual. Hammett in this book tries to do far more than write a couple of hundred pages and then tell "whodunit."

●

But then Hammett hit a slump in his Hollywood career. None of the film companies was interested in optioning *The Dain Curse*, and he found no immediate takers for *The Glass Key*. In 1932 Hammett cashed in on the popularity of *The Maltese Falcon* and quickly wrote three short stories about Sam Spade. He did not direct them to the pulp market, but sold them to the slicks. Pulps — so called because they were printed on the cheapest wood pulp paper — were in his past. Slicks — so called because of the slick coating on the paper — were in his present, and paid much, much more. He is rumored to have received around one thousand dollars each for these new Spade tales. Those were his only stories for the year.

Hammett's last active burst of fiction writing came in 1933, as he somewhat desperately tried to come up with some properties which would appeal to the Hollywood producers, and he made several attempts at short stories

which would take him out of the crime genre — one of
these stories, "Night Shade," is considered by Hammett
admirers as an example of his style at its peak. Far less
satisfying is a short novel he serialized in three parts in
Liberty, *Woman in the Dark*, done in the same style as
The Glass Key, even to the heroine's name always
appearing in the narration as Luise Fischer, both names,
never by one or the other, but lacking the suggestion of
unspoken meaning with which Hammett invested the
story of Ned Beaumont. Almost certainly Hammett wrote
Woman in the Dark with an eye toward a pickup by
Hollywood, in addition to the thousands *Liberty* paid for
it.

By 1933, despite the royalties from his novels and the
thousands of dollars made from his new stories and
screenwriting, Hammett suddenly found himself broke.
He spent money on women, parties, drinking, and
gambling as fast as it came in, and in 1933 it was not
coming in fast enough anymore. To appreciate the amount
of money Hammett was running through, you must
consider that in the fall of 1929, the stock market crashed,
plunging the country into the Great Depression. The
newspaper columnist Russell Baker, in his Pulitzer Prize
winning autobiography *Growing Up* (1982), writes about
that time, when he was a child. Nineteen-thirty and thirty-
one were bad years, but 1932, he said, was "the bleakest
year of the Depression." Baker's father had died, leaving
him and his mother destitute. One of her brothers took
them in. Baker said he was a "salesman for a soft-drink
bottler in Newark . . . wore pearl-gray spats, detachable
collars, and a three piece suit, . . . and took in threadbare
relatives." His uncle did this on "an income of $30 a
week." During the Depression, if you were making $1500
a year, you were pretty well off. The $8,500 Warner
Brothers paid for *The Maltese Falcon* alone, a seemingly
trivial amount by today's standards, could have supported
several families in style through those years. Hammett
burned through the money.

With Hellman in New York, Hammett went to earth in
the Hotel Sutton on East 56th Street, managed by their
friend Nathanael West, who would go on to write the
classic novels *Miss Lonelyhearts* and *The Day of the
Locust*. West's brother-in-law, the humorist S. J.

From the pulps to the slicks

Perelman, described the hotel in the memoir *The Last Laugh* (1981): "The decor of all the rooms was identical — fireproof early-American, impervious to the whim of guests who might succumb to euphoria, despair or drunkenness." In her memoirs Lillian Hellman said that West would let his broke writer pals run up a rent bill under assumed names, then check those names out, telling the owner the guests had skipped out, meanwhile registering new names without having to disturb the literati.

With himself and Hellman as the models for his heroes, and using the experiences he had had spending his money, Hammett settled in at the Sutton for what would be his last major creative work: a new detective novel, *The Thin Man*, said to have been written in two weeks flat. A slick commercial effort, more akin to the mysteries of S. S. Van Dine than to his own hard-boiled fictions, *The Thin Man* instantly became Hammett's bestselling book. The wise-cracking, hard-drinking husband and wife sleuths Nick and Nora Charles would carry him financially for years to come. Hammett dedicated the novel to Hellman, and it clearly reflects their life together in New York living off the Hollywood money, though in the story Nick Charles has retired from his job with the Trans-Continental Detective Agency to manage the millions inherited by Nora. Another personal allusion in the book is the dog Asta, named after the dog owned by S. J. Perelman's wife Laura.

The Thin Man appeared in *Redbook*, December 1933, and Hammett and Hellman used the magazine payment to cover a few weeks spent in Miami, followed by more weeks in spring and summer of 1934 relaxing in a fishing camp in the Florida Keys. Alfred A. Knopf brought out the hardback in January that year.

Once more, Hammett was hot. The W. S. Van Dyke film of *The Thin Man*, starring William Powell and Myrna Loy as Nick and Nora, appeared before the year was out; M-G-M paid $20,000 for the screen rights. RKO Radio Pictures picked up *The Woman in the Dark*, starring Fay Wray of *King Kong* fame in the title role. King Features Syndicate hired Hammett to create a comic strip character and write continuity as competition for *Dick Tracy*; he came up with a tough unnamed government man known only as *Secret Agent X-9*, with the panels drawn by Alex Raymond (more famous today for the science-fiction strip *Flash Gordon*). Hammett is thought to have written two long episodes which appeared in 1934 and 1935, and to have plotted — possibly — a couple more. The pay sometimes is reported to have been $500 per week.

In 1935 Universal Pictures brought out *Mister Dynamite*, adapted from an original screen story by Hammett called "On the Make." This film is set in San Francisco (though filmed in Hollywood on sets), and much of the action occurs in the St. Francis Hotel. Edmund Lowe stars as the detective named Dynamite, a roguish fellow who wears white gloves most of the time and leaves no fingerprints behind. At one point this vehicle was intended as another starring role for William Powell, in which he would play Sam Spade *gone crooked*. Protest from Warner Brothers over rights sidetracked that possibility.

Also in 1935 a film made from *The Glass Key* was released by Paramount, starring George Raft as Ned Beaumont. In 1936 Warners tried again with *The Maltese Falcon*. The 1931 version with Ricardo Cortez had bombed, and so did attempt number two, *Satan Met a Lady*, which features neither Sam Spade nor the falcon. Instead of a fat man there is a fat woman. Instead of slimy little Joel Cairo, you find in the role the tall English actor Arthur Treacher, famous for playing butlers ("*My word!*"). Some genius in Hollywood has them after Roland's Horn of Plenty, filled with jewels, from French (yeah, right) rather than Maltese legends. The movie stars Bette Davis. She said it was the worst dog she ever made in Hollywood.

●

By 1934, with successes cutting through the book market, the newspapers, and film, Hammett without doubt was the uncrowned king of the crime story in America. But for the easy money to be made from mysteries, though, he might have abdicated his throne that year. Hammett had become tired of writing detective stories, and had his eye on other forms.

The social reality from which his hard-boiled fiction sprang had not changed that much, though he had. Pinkerton operatives were still busting heads as strikebreakers and crime was as popular as ever. The critics who think Hammett's fiction too violent need only look at the headlines the year his last novel appeared to see that *The Thin Man* is a relatively gentle read. Reality only matched *Red Harvest* more as Bonnie Parker and Clyde Barrow died in a hail of bullets May 23, 1934, followed by John Dillinger in July, Pretty Boy Floyd in October, and Baby Face Nelson in November. Ma Barker stayed alive until January 1935, then she too died in an epic gun battle with the law. And in San Francisco an island in the middle of the bay was converted to a new use in September 1934, as Alcatraz — "The Super Prison for Super Criminals" — opened its gates for customers.

Hammett's preoccupations were elsewhere. In 1934 Lillian Hellman's first produced play, *The Children's Hour*, came to the theater. She said that Hammett suggested to her the incident of teachers tried for lesbianism as ripe for drama; he may even have been considering working up a play or a novel on the subject himself before turning the idea over to her. Knopf was waiting for Hammett's next novel, but he did not expect a mystery. Hammett was planning a mainstream novel, perhaps something like his drinking buddy William Faulkner was writing, or his ex-landlord Nathanael "Pep" West. He knew the major writers of the day, and his expectations for his writing came to be measured against what they were producing. He could possibly have sat down at the typewriter and knocked out eighty or so books about Sam Spade at the same time his fellow *Black Mask* writer Erle Stanley Gardner was writing his long series of books about the lawyer Perry Mason, but he did not care to do that. Hammett came to feel that he had done all he legitimately could do with the mystery story without beginning to repeat himself.

He announced titles of his mainstream novels over the next years. *There Was a Young Man. The Hunting Boy. The Valley Sheep are Fatter.* He got a few pages into some of these novels before freezing up. Once *The Thin Man* and three short stories saw print in 1934, no other new novels or stories by Hammett would appear for the rest of his life. Knopf waited impatiently a few years, and then dropped Hammett's contract.

By 1935 Hammett had stopped writing for *Secret Agent X-9*, but it was this innocuous assignment that initially brought his name to the attention of the FBI. J. Edgar Hoover happened to notice that X-9, in the comic strip a free-floating agent of some faceless branch of the government, had started out as a "G-Man," one of his boys. He requested a background check on Hammett. As Hammett's politics moved increasingly to the left, the FBI file on him grew, and by the time of his death it stacked up quite evenly with a New York City phone book.

The movie *After the Thin Man*, second in the series of six films, appeared in 1936. M-G-M brought Hammett back to Hollywood to work on a screen treatment, to be followed by a screenplay written by others. They hired him for $2000 a week for something like ten weeks to write on the project, during which time he stayed drunk and made the social rounds. Then came five weeks more at $2000 a week, with no screen story, followed by five more weeks at half pay, $1000 a week — loose figures, but close enough to the actuality.

In this period Hammett knew everyone; as Hellman said, for a season or two he was the hottest thing in both New York and Hollywood. He met former Ziegfield Follies star Fanny Brice, and Orson Welles. With Hellman he visited the Perelmans on their farm, and with Hellman he went out drinking with William Faulkner when he came to New York. Hellman recalls one dinner party at a restaurant with Hammett and F. Scott Fitzgerald and Ernest Hemingway, where Hemingway mercilessly browbeat Fitzgerald until Hammett could stand it no more and told him to lay off. Hemingway asked the former detective if he wanted to arm wrestle, and Hammett told him he should go out into the parking lot and "roll a hoop." Jerome Weidman, author of *I Can Get It for You Wholesale* and later the Pulitzer Prize winning play *Fiorello!* about New York City mayor LaGuardia, met Hammett in 1937 and said everyone expected a new novel out from him any day.

In 1937 Hammett and Hellman rented an island cottage off South Norwalk, Connecticut, where she worked on her play *The Little Foxes*. Hammett, who apparently kept trying to create a noncrime novel well into the 1940s, if he was writing during that time, sat balked, staring at blank sheets. The true creative outlet for his energies from that point on would be Hellman and her plays, as he began to act as a first reader for her. In her memoirs Hellman gives Hammett much credit for instilling in her an attitude which pushed for only the very best work, summed up in his observation about something she had just written: *You can't let this be published or performed — this is* worse *than bad — it's only* half-good. If he was stalled on his own writing, nonetheless he was there in support of Hellman — from the suggestion of the trial on which she based *The Children's Hour* to a detailed criticism of *The Autumn Garden*, first performed in 1951, a play for which Hellman credits him with contributing a pivotal speech in the last act spoken by the character Ben Griggs. This speech ends with what today only can be taken as a stark autobiographical statement from a writer whose last prose work had appeared in 1934: "I've frittered myself away."

●

Later in 1937 and into 1938 Hammett moved back into the Beverly Wilshire, returning to Hollywood for a third film about Nick and Nora Charles. Savvy to the possible problems they might have with Hammett after his delays with the screen treatment for the second *Thin Man* film, M-G-M signed him on with a contract with increasing benefits — the synopsis would earn $5,000, acceptance of the idea for the movie outlined in the synopsis would earn $10,000, and a finished screen treatment would pull in another $20,000. The third in the series, *Another Thin Man*, appeared in 1939, the last time Hammett personally had anything to do with the characters.

While he was in Hollywood M-G-M also made Hammett an offer of $40,000 for all further dramatic rights to Nick and Nora, which he accepted with only one change — he would keep radio rights, since Old Gold cigarettes were even then offering him $500 a week for a radio series. Hammett had grown as tired of Nick and Nora as he had of his old work in *Black Mask*, which may suggest some self-disgust over his inability to escape from crime fiction into the literary mainstream. Ernest Hemingway in the autobiographical *Death in the Afternoon* (1932) wrote that he had his wife read to him from *The Dain Curse*, but by that time Hammett was dismissing *The Dain Curse* as "a silly story." When he sold film rights to Nick and Nora Charles, he could write, "Maybe there are better writers in the world but nobody ever invented a more insufferably smug pair of characters. They can't take that away from me even for $40,000."

Hammett returned to Baltimore in February 1939 with Lillian Hellman to attend the opening of *The Little Foxes*. Her successes for the stage enabled Hellman to purchase one hundred and thirty acres, dubbed Hardscrabble Farm, in Pleasantville, New York. Hammett often stopped there through the next decade, though he kept his own apartments in New York City.

In 1941 a young screenwriter on the Warner Brothers lot wanted a shot at directing. The Warners had no problems with that, as long as he kept the costs down, shot on the backlots, got the thing in on a fast schedule. They already had all rights in the property paid for, since John Huston wanted to direct a new version of *The Maltese Falcon*, confident that no one would remember the two earlier versions, which he — of a similar mind as Bette Davis — dismissed as "dogs."

Huston's first film follows the novel closely, and especially is faithful to Hammett's dialogue. This adherence to the novel may have been accidental. In interviews for TV years later Huston said that he was so nervous about directing that he felt lucky to have such a professional cast, with Humphrey Bogart and Mary Astor and Peter Lorre practically directing themselves. Sidney Greenstreet was making his movie debut, but he had acted on the stage for many years. One suspects that Huston, as a screenwriter himself, may have wanted to rewrite the material more extensively than he did, but had his attention diverted by his job as director. The desire at Warners to keep it cheap may have been the crucial factor. In *Hammett: A Life at the Edge* (1983), William F. Nolan recounts a story told by Allen Rivkin about how Huston, realizing he would be busy as director, asked him to be coscreenwriter for the project. Rivkin said that

Huston had his secretary at Warners type the novel into blocks of scenes with dialogue. Jack Warner saw this typescript, okayed it, and told Huston to start filming. Rivkin was out of a job, and pressure was on to get the project made.

Using stock documentary footage of the new bridges over the bay and downtown San Francisco as viewed from the waterfront to set the scene, Huston shot the rest of the movie at Warners — freezeframe the shot where *La Paloma* comes into dock and you will see the logo "Port of Los Angeles" for the piers. Bogart came in every morning from his home at 8787 Shoreham Road. Originally Huston had wanted George Raft in the role of Sam Spade, but Raft, then at the peak of his career, was not willing to trust his future on any untried director such as John Huston with a property like *The Maltese Falcon*, which had bombed twice. Raft's refusal opened the part for Bogart, who was just beginning to rise again at Warner Brothers after playing Raft's kid brother in *They Drive by Night* and co-starring opposite Ida Lupino in *High Sierra*, scripted by John Huston. Bogart had become typecast at Warners for years after his role as Duke Mantee in *The Petrified Forest*, playing a succession of shyster lawyers and gangsters. In *The Maltese Falcon* he got his first opportunity to portray the hero, the leading man — and the part as Sam Spade catapulted him to superstardom.

Although Hammett made no money from this third film version of the *Falcon*, it signaled the opening of a decade in which he was without rival as the most famous mystery writer in America. M-G-M kept Nick and Nora before the public in *Shadow of the Thin Man* (1941), *The Thin Man Goes Home* (1944), and *Song of the Thin Man* (1947). Paramount brought Ned Beaumont back to the screen in the person of Alan Ladd in a 1942 remake of *The Glass Key*.

The airwaves were alive with Hammett characterizations, with *The Adventures of the Thin Man* beginning in 1941 and running to 1942; interrupted by the second World War, in 1948 Nick and Nora returned over NBC in *The New Adventures of the Thin Man*. In 1946 Hammett merchandized *The Adventures of Sam Spade*, sponsored by Wildroot Cream Oil for the hair, with

Howard Duff as the voice of Sam Spade ("Effie, take a memo...."). Warner Brothers sued him over this show, alleging they owned the dramatic rights to Sam Spade, but the courts decided otherwise, so that Hammett, if unrewarded by the box office take from the Bogart version, nonetheless profited by the high profile of his detective, with some accounts figuring his weekly fee for the radio rights at a thousand or even two thousand dollars. The show ran for years, with one of the most interesting episodes reuniting Spade with Gutman and Cairo in "The Adventure of the Kandy Tooth" — Kandy as in Ceylon. In 1946 Hammett also created a character expressly made for radio, in a loose sense a continuation of his heavyset Continental Op and a fine counterpart to the Thin Man series. This show began: "There he goes! Into that drug store. He's stepping on the scales.... Weight: 237 pounds. Fortune: Danger! Who is he...? *The Fat Man*...!" The sponsor for *The Fat Man* series had to be the most appropriate in the entire history of radio, with the adventures of Brad Runyon, a.k.a. the Fat Man, brought to the listeners by Pepto Bismol. Some accounts have Hammett as script supervisor for this show, others suggest — more believably — that after he sold the idea he had nothing more to do with it. The most amazing version has it that Hammett provided only three words, *the — fat — man*, for the show, earning a fee of $60,000 — $20,000 a word.

Hammett also allowed Ellery Queen to assemble some of his old pulp fiction for paperback publication, beginning in 1945 with three story collections, *The Adventures of Sam Spade*, *The Continental Op*, and *The Return of the Continental Op*. The royalties from these books could have rivaled in no way the money Hammett was making from his radio shows, but it *was* money coming in, free and easy. And Hammett, apparently, felt no hesitation over these books appearing to muddle the reputation he had built up with his five hardcover novels from Knopf. Like a great many other people in the early days of the paperback or pocket book, Hammett does not seem to have regarded them as "real books." Rather, they were disposable reading, inconsequential, and unlike the real books which came out in hardback, in no danger of being taken seriously.

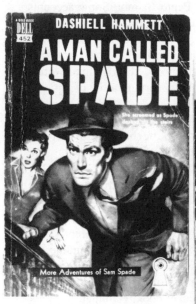

Dell Mapback Editions, 1940s

When she assembled the first hardcover collection of Hammett's *Black Mask* tales in *The Big Knockover* (1966), Hellman noted that "by publishing them at all, I have done what Hammett did not want to do: he turned down offers to republish the stories, although I never knew the reason and never asked." Surely she refers to hardcover issues, because Frederic Dannay as "Ellery Queen" eventually brought out almost all of Hammett's pulp shorts in no less than nine paperback collections.

•

During the thirties, in New York and Hollywood, Hammett drifted out of his state of being politically unaware, cause unknown. Whether it was residual guilt over his years as a strikebreaker and the suggested complicity in the lynching of Frank Little, or perhaps a spark ignited while listening to the political rhetoric passing about the intellectual circles he moved in, may never be determined. Historically, though, Hammett's activism seems to have been occasioned by an event which brought many people in that era into the political arena — the rise of Adolf Hitler and the Nazis.

Completely aside from the elements of Marxist politics that began to appeal to him, Hammett recognized Hitler as a genuine threat. He spoke at anti-Nazi rallies and began to contribute to political causes, which brought him back to the active attention of the FBI. His concern over the rise of the fascist nations spurred him to finish the only film assignment he considered important, and then prompted him at the age of forty-eight to enlist in the army as America entered World War II.

Early in 1942 Hammett signed on with producer Hal B. Wallis at Warner Brothers to adapt Lillian Hellman's play *Watch on the Rhine* for the screen, and agreed to do so "in record time." He wired on April 13th that he would finish the script that week if he did not break a leg. His wire on April 23rd communicated his activity in one word: "Done." Hammett took this assignment seriously, both because of his respect for Hellman's material and for the message the play — and thus the movie — put before the public. *Watch on the Rhine*, during all his years in and out of Hollywood, was his only screenplay credit, the rest being stories for the screen that other writers finished. The credit reads *Screenplay by Dashiell Hammett — with additional scenes and dialogue by Lillian Hellman*. The movie came out in 1943, directed by Herman Shumlin, starring Paul Lukas and Bette Davis. Lukas won an Oscar as Best Actor of the year for his performance. Hammett's screenplay was nominated for an Oscar, but did not win.

The antifascist message of that movie clearly was important to Hammett, but he realized it was not enough just to make a statement. To Hellman's disbelief, and against her protests, he enlisted as a private in the army in September, 1942. Initially he was refused induction. When the doctor asked about the scars that appeared on his lungs in the X-rays, Hammett said that they came from TB, although he had been cured by 1927. As the war effort stepped up, they became less choosy, and soon Hammett was stationed stateside, but felt he was wasting his time with busy-work while the war raged in Europe and the Pacific.

Hammett put in a request to be moved to a combat zone, which was refused. It is unclear whether or not the officials in the army had any reservations about him because of his leftist political beliefs. Possibly the most amusing aspect of his FBI file is the fact that when he joined the army, the FBI completely lost track of where he was for most of his time in the service. They were keeping an eye on Dashiell Hammett, but he enlisted under the name Samuel D. Hammett, and just disappeared.

Taking the matter through channels, Hammett asked for a medical reason why he could not be sent to a combat zone. He was told his teeth were too bad. He went to the dentist on the base, had *all* of his teeth pulled, and shortly after was transferred to the islands of Adak and Kiska in the Aleutian chain, where he made the rank of corporal and was put in charge of the servicemen's newspaper, *The Adakian*. He and Corporal Robert Colodny during this time wrote the booklet *The Battle of the Aleutians: A Graphic History 1942-1943*, published by the army Intelligence Section in 1944. Ironically, given his efforts to place himself in a combat zone, Hammett missed what little action occurred in the Aleutians, and only got to write a book about it.

Hammett loved army life in the Aleutians. The much younger men he was stationed with called him "Grandpop" or "Pop," asked his advice, borrowed money. In all apparent seriousness he sent Lillian Hellman letters telling her about what a great place the Aleutians were, and how after the war was over they would have to buy land there, build a place to live. She was never to take him up on the offer. Hammett glamourized life in the army as he had never glamourized detective work, with even a dismal march to the latrines against the crushing winds made to sound epic.

The jazz sax player Bud Freeman of Chicago was one of the troops stationed with Hammett, and he recalled him as "a super guy. He used to give two lectures a week on China. . . . It was like going to school. He had a lot of knowledge and was a wonderful man." Referring to the editorials Hammett wrote for *The Adakian*, Freeman said, "I remember that he would favor the progress of the Russian troops, our allies, and rarely ever mentioned anything about the American forces. And, as I recall, the general of the Alaskan command came down to see him about that. The general asked him why he didn't write of the progress of American forces. Dashiell said, 'Well, sir, this paper has a policy not to publish any ads.' "

●

Hammett spent the last few months of his army service in Anchorage, and for some reason soured on the idea he had had of simply staying in the army. He left the service by September, 1945, and went back to civilian life, with the radio shows of Sam Spade and the Fat Man paying his way.

In addition to spending his money on good times, Hammett increasingly became a contributor to leftist causes. He gave thousands of dollars to various groups, signed petitions, appeared at rallies. Beginning in 1947, he taught a class in creative writing for the Jefferson

School of Social Services in New York. Frederic Dannay
would be one of the writers Hammett brought in to speak
to his classes.

In *Shadow Man* Richard Layman notes that in 1949
Hammett hired a secretary to help him with miscellaneous
chores, as he decided to start writing again. But his
typewriter seldom was engaged, and his secretary recalled
that they would sit silent for hours at a stretch, reading. In
her introduction to *The Big Knockover* Hellman spoke of
that period beginning about 1948, noting, "good as it is,
productivity is not the only proof of a serious life, and
now, more than ever, he sat down to read. He read
everything and anything." His secretary said that
Hammett, as his apartment piled up with books, would
often burn some of them in the fireplace, and give more
away to clear out the space. Also, he would receive
requests for jacket blurbs; Layman mentions one from
Agatha Christie's publisher, on which he says Hammett
declined comment. One of the few endorsements he
seems to have given was a blurb for the 1948 English
edition of *The Best Short Stories of M. P. Shiel*, where he
stated that the author of that novel which had so gripped
the Continental Op a couple of decades before was "a
magician."

After the war Hammett finally bought a house near
Los Angeles for his wife Josephine. He spent six
months there with her and their daughters in 1950, lured
back to Hollywood for the final time by the promise of
relatively easy money for more crime writing for the
screen. The project for which he took an advance was
more ambitious than most: the director William Wyler
was developing a film for Paramount called *Detective
Story*, to star Kirk Douglas, and he wanted Hammett to
do the screenplay. In this same period Hammett also
talked with Alfred Hitchcock about working on one of
his films, but that fell through, and Raymond Chandler
would be the *Black Mask* alumnus who wrote for the
1951 *Strangers on a Train*. The deal with Wyler also
fell through. Hammett found that he could not write,
and he returned the advance he had received and bowed
out of the project. In an interview with the *Los Angeles
Times* during his visit, Hammett commented on the
tough school of detective writing of which he was the

primary mover. He said, "This hard-boiled stuff is a menace."

In 1950, the only literary project he found himself interested in was the progress of Hellman's play *The Autumn Garden*, though he did manage to write a short introduction for George Marion's book *The Communist Trial*.

In 1951 Hammett's own Marxist political beliefs came to trial. From about 1946, when he was elected president of the group, Hammett had been associated with and active in the causes of the Civil Rights Congress, which had Communist affiliations. Whether or not Hammett was a card-carrying member of any branch of the American Communist Party is unknown. Hellman in her memoirs says that she did not know if he was or not. Even the FBI, for all the data they piled up on Hammett, could not determine that point to their satisfaction. Finally, the opinion of the FBI seemed to be that Hammett was so important to the Communist Party in America that they would not let him join publicly, feeling he was of greater use as a free agent.

When the water got hot during the McCarthy years Hammett was serving as chairman of the bail bond fund for the Civil Rights Congress. Four Communists released on bail from that fund skipped out, and Hammett and three other men connected with it were pulled into court. This incident was used as an excuse to ask for names of contributors to the fund, which were not part of the CRC's public records. The man who had gone into court before Hammett had refused to cooperate and had been sentenced to six months in prison for contempt. Likewise, Hammett refused to cooperate with the inquiry; he took the Fifth Amendment repeatedly when pressed on his association with the Civil Rights Congress, invoking his rights under the Fifth about eighty times before the judge tired of it and sentenced him to six months in prison for contempt. When asked at the sentencing if he had anything to say as to why judgment should not be pronounced upon him, Hammett said, "Not a thing."

On July 10, 1951, he was put into West Street Jail in New York City. From there he was transferred to a federal penitentiary in West Virginia and then to a prison in Kentucky. He got a month off for good behavior and was freed December 11, 1951.

Hellman wrote that when she met Hammett at the airport after his release, he stumbled going down the stairs from the airplane, and was never to become well again. The stay in prison, the years in the Aleutian chain, his history of heavy smoking matched by heavy drinking, the TB from years back: all the factors which undermined his health began to overtake him.

Coming out of prison, Hammett found himself one of a growing number of writers and artists facing a blacklist. He was no longer active in screenwriting, so he could not be fired by a studio or refused work by others, but he saw his name fade away just the same. Commercial sponsors in the McCarthy era were afraid to be seen connected with a "Communist writer." Hammett's lucrative radio shows went off the air and Hollywood shied off from optioning any more of his stories. A movie from Universal International in 1951 of *The Fat Man*, featuring J. Scott Smart as Brad Runyon and a young Rock Hudson, would be the last film related to his work released in his lifetime. In 1952 Ellery Queen edited an eighth collection of Hammett's pulp writing under the title *Woman in the Dark*; the ninth and final Queen gathering, *A Man Named Thin*, would not see print until 1962, after Hammett had been dead for a year.

Only the witty martini-downing sleuths Nick and Nora Charles were able to survive their connection with Hammett. In 1937 when he sold M-G-M the dramatic rights for $40,000, Hammett dismissed them as "insufferably smug," but said theirs was a "charming fable of how Nick loved Nora and Nora loved Nick and everything was just one big laugh in the midst of other people's trials and tribulations." So true. Starring Peter Lawford, *The Thin Man* came to the new medium of television in the years when all other Hammett properties were untouchable. Because he had sold film rights — Hammett had not anticipated TV — he made nothing from this show.

Hammett desperately could have used the money from the TV series. On the heels of his release from prison the Internal Revenue Service looked into his tax situation, and figured he owed unpaid taxes plus penalties to the tune of about $140,000. They froze his royalties and bank account, seizing the money that was available, but Hammett still owed more, and in the face of the blacklist the money stopped rolling in. For some years the only funds he had free from the IRS was a percentage investment he made in Arthur Miller's play *The Death of a Salesman*, which brought in roughly $80 each year. But for the fact that Hellman and other friends paid his rent and bought him food, Hammett's last years could have been much more desperate than they were.

In 1952 his friends Dr. Sam and Helen Rosen offered him the four-room gatehouse cottage of their place in Katonah, New York, with the $75 per month rent paid by Hellman. Hammett piled the place up with the books and gadgets Hellman mentions he kept around, as well as a great deal of unanswered mail. Here he sat at the typewriter for one last try at one of the mainstream novels he had been thinking and talking about. It was called *Tulip*, and the fragment he managed to finish was first published by Hellman in *The Big Knockover* in 1966, the only non-Continental Op tale in that collection.

Tulip is so clearly autobiographical that details from it have been lifted and applied to Hammett's life in the various biographies. The story concerns a character named "Pop," who like Hammett had had TB, had been on Kiska, had started to write while in San Francisco. This was Hammett, of course, even to the inclusion of a bizarre book review of Arthur Edward Waite's 1924 *The Brotherhood of the Rosy Cross*, on the Rosicrucian Order, the sort of off-trail book Hammett sought out and the kind from which he first learned of the falcon sent to Charles V by the knights of Malta.

The main manuscript fragment of *Tulip* ends after sixty or so pages with the brutal observation: "If you are tired you ought to rest, I think, and not try to fool yourself and your customers with colored bubbles." Hammett wrote four short paragraphs for the end of the projected book, in which the character Tulip says to Pop about the manuscript Pop has been working on, "I hurried through it this first time, but I'll read it again kind of carefully if you want me to." But Hammett never filled in the rest of the manuscript.

●

In 1953 Hammett was called before the televised Senate Internal Subcommittee hearings personally conducted by Senator Joseph McCarthy with Senator John McClellan and the lawyer for the subcommittee, Roy Cohn. Each time they asked Hammett about any Communist ties he may have had, he took the Fifth. The final question from McCarthy is today famous:

> Mr. Hammett, if you were spending, as we are, over a hundred million dollars a year on an information program allegedly for the purpose of fighting Communism, and if you were in charge of that program to fight Communism, would you purchase the works of some 75 Communist authors and distribute their works throughout the world . . . ?

McCarthy referred to books bought by the government for its libraries for servicemen. Hammett replied:

> Well, I think — of course, I don't know — if I were fighting Communism, I don't think I would do it by giving people any books at all.

McCarthy said, "From an author, that sounds unusual." At that point, Hammett's works were pulled from government libraries, but soon were put back when President Dwight D. Eisenhower made a statement to the press that he personally would not have removed them from the shelves.

By the time he was questioned by McCarthy, Hammett had nothing more to lose. He had stood up for his beliefs, and like so many others who stood up for their beliefs against the forces of HUAC, he had been crushed. Unlike many of the others, however, Hammett did not whine about his treatment; interviewed in 1957 by the *Washington Daily News*, he sardonically mentioned that he kept no less than three typewriters in his Katonah cottage, "to remind myself I was once a writer." And of his imprisonment for contempt of court in 1951, he stated, "I found the crooks had not changed since I was a Pinkerton man. Going to prison was like going home."

Going home. For many Hammett fans, his stance during the McCarthy period is vindication for the years when he turned away from his hard-boiled stories, because Hammett facing the enemy in the 1950s could have been the Op or Sam Spade facing the enemy in his fiction — the attitude was the same, the code was the same. Ultimately, Hammett held true to the philosophy he put forth in his stories. Whatever he may have thought about knocking out the *Black Mask* junk in the 1920s or how many times he dismissed it later, in his stories it is obvious he was not kidding around — he personally meant what he said. When the chance came for Hammett to cooperate with the people who wanted to shove him around, he could have cooperated and kept his money, remained insufferably smug even as others faced their trials, but he did not. If he did not like it, he nonetheless took it. And refused the opportunities they gave him to beg.

●

In increasingly poor health, Hammett gave up his cottage later in 1957 and moved in with Hellman. From then until his death he lived in her New York apartment in 63 East 82nd Street or her place on Martha's Vineyard. The last couple of years he spent as a near invalid, watching TV for hours at a time.

On January 10, 1961, Hammett died in Lenox Hill Hospital in New York City — cancer of the lungs was the major contributing cause of death.

Hammett had requested that his body be buried in Arlington National Cemetery. He liked the army, feeling it was one of the very few social institutions in America in which there was some attempt to enforce social equality. The last letter in his FBI file dates from early 1961, as J. Edgar Hoover personally issued a statement opposing Hammett's interment in Arlington, and wondering if something could not be done to prevent the burial of this Communist in the national graveyard. But Joseph McCarthy had died in the mid-fifties, and with him went the Communist witchhunt of that day. Hammett had served in both World Wars and his burial in Arlington went ahead despite Hoover's objections.

Hammett's importance in the fiction and film of crime and violence, the noir fiction and film that followed World War I and continues unbroken to this day, cannot be overestimated. His work paved the way for Raymond Chandler's romantic private-eye stories set in a Los Angeles bathed in heat and scented with jacaranda blossoms. He provided Bogart with the pivotal role of his career, and the Bogart cult, as widespread today as ever, has deep affinities with the cult for Hammett. The appearance of his novels and stories in paperback recreated the excitement of their appearances in *Black Mask*, inspiring in the forties and fifties new generations of writers to try the hard-boiled arena — inspiring new writers today.

His influence has spread far beyond the bounds of the detective novel, so that he now is coming to be more and more placed not with his fellow pulp fictioneers in *Black Mask*, but with Faulkner and Hemingway and other major authors of his time, a standard.

In his stories and novels, the majority of them written in San Francisco, Hammett did what only a handful of writers have done: he created a mythic popular culture figure in the character of Sam Spade, the hard-boiled detective, and created works of fiction which stand, more than half a century later, with the best of their kind.

Don Herron on Tour

DASHIELL HAMMETT TOUR

Samuel Dashiell Hammett arrived in San Francisco about June, 1921, and left in the fall of 1929. He began writing in this city, finishing all the stories and novels in his long series featuring the Continental Op, as well as his single most famous work, *The Maltese Falcon*. In the tour which follows you can see the major sites of interest to the Hammett fan: all the known residences, scenes from his job with Pinkerton, and the majority of locales from his novel about Sam Spade, including the deadend alley where Spade's partner Miles Archer met swift death in the night-fog, and the Hammett hangout John's Grill. Easily walked in two to three hours — or driven in a half hour — the tour starts in the Civic Center, a block from the BART and Muni Metro Station, loops along the edges of the Tenderloin, over Nob Hill, then down toward Union Square, and finishes near the cable car turntable and the Powell Street BART Station.

Begin where Larkin Street crosses McAllister, with the large building of gray stone on the southeast corner:

1 200 LARKIN

This building was dedicated in February 1917 as San Francisco's new main library, and Hammett, a prolific reader most of his life, made much use of it. In an interview with his wife and older daughter Mary Jane published in the November 4, 1975 issue of *City of San Francisco* magazine, Josephine Dolan Hammett recalled that he particularly frequented the library when he was sick, walking to this building every afternoon. The Hammetts lived for about five years in an apartment building at 620 Eddy, just three blocks up Larkin. The walks may have served as constitutionals for Hammett when the TB he had contracted in the army in World War I returned to plague his health during his first years in San Francisco. In the early twenties Hammett simply was not making enough money to buy many books on his own, and in any case, seems to have been by temperament a natural library user. Check the book out, read it, return it. His younger daughter, named Josephine after her mother, said that once when Hammett signed out of a hotel he had been living in, he left behind over fifty books for room service to dispose of. But the hotel had the books packed and shipped to him. Hammett received the crate and was baffled as to the possible contents. When he opened it he could not believe it. Why had they forwarded *these books*? He had *already read* these books.

In the mid-1990s this building is scheduled to be converted from use as the main library into a new home for the Asian Art Museum, with a newly constructed library facility to open near the close of 1995, adjacent in the 100 block of Larkin. The modern library will complete the plans for buildings to enclose the Civic Center that were envisioned after the destruction wrought by the 1906 earthquake and fire. A new era for the San Francisco library will begin, but it is the old building at 200 Larkin that will hold the memory of Dashiell Hammett in the twenties, of his stops here in his lifelong quest among books.

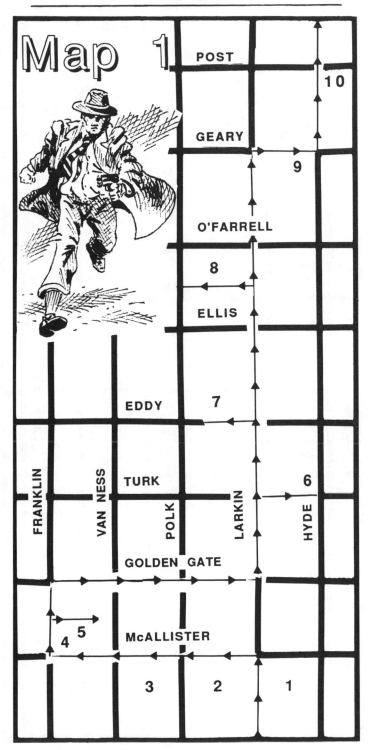

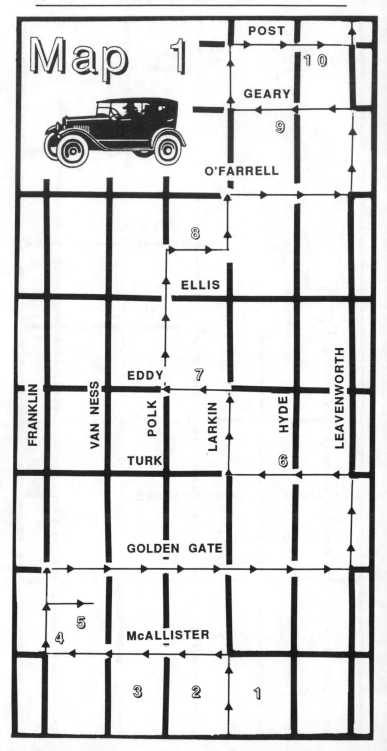

Across Larkin Street from the old library building you'll see:

2 CIVIC CENTER PARK

In the *City* interview, given when she was eighty years old, Josephine Hammett mentioned bringing their first baby, Mary Jane, "to the park" — this park, conveniently close to their Eddy Street apartment. Mary Jane was born October 15, 1921, and her sister Josephine came along May 24, 1926, near the end of the Hammetts' residence on Eddy. Jo Hammett said that their mother often took them to parks, sometimes on extended excursions to Golden Gate Park or Fleishhacker Pool next to the Pacific Ocean. Josephine Dolan was originally from Anaconda, Montana, and her younger daughter said that in many ways she remained a country girl, with a country view of child raising, which is to say, if you want healthy children, get them outdoors into the fresh air. Even in the twenties fresh air seemed to be lacking on Eddy Street, so Josephine — or Jose — Hammett would get her girls up in the morning, feed them breakfast, dress them, bring them down to this park. They would go home for lunch, then come back until it was dinner time. On the bitter cold days for the tour, I have an image of these little girls, spending half their young lives freezing here in this park.

In the interview, Mrs. Hammett stated that when she brought the girls to the park in the afternoon to play, Hammett stayed home and cooked supper. She said he liked to cook hamburger with lettuce and when they could afford it, ground round. In the early twenties they probably could not often afford ground round. She believed that Hammett was earning, as a Pinkerton operative in 1921, about $105 per month, while rent for their apartment was $45 a month. His initial writing for the pulp magazines, which began late in 1922, could not have paid much, because the pulps, on average, paid about 1¢ a word for material. Two ways existed for making better money as a pulp fictioneer: you could sit down at the typewriter and pound out millions of words a year, and many writers did; or *via* the appeal of your work to the readers you could slowly work your way up to better word rates, to 4¢ and 5¢ and — for a select few — even 6¢ a word. Hammett with only six novel-length works and slightly more than one hundred short stories to his credit was by no means prolific compared to other writers for the pulps, such as Max Brand, who turned out well over a million words per annum year after year, or Erle Stanley Gardner, who wrote over eighty novels about his character Perry Mason alone, or the amazing Walter Gibson, who under the name Maxwell Grant was writing weekly novels about *The Shadow* and before he stopped had knocked out over three hundred adventures of that macabre crimefighter. Soon the appearance of Hammett's name on the cover of *Black Mask* would guarantee a 20% increase in sales for that issue, and he could ask for a raise in word rates. When he hit 3¢ about 1924 the editor at *Black Mask* refused to pay him more — it was bad business to pay your writers too much money — so Hammett sold his next couple of stories to a rival magazine, and *Black Mask* bought him back. As the veteran pulp writer E. Hoffmann Price once told me, based on his experience of selling some 600 stories to a wide variety of pulp magazines, the only way you could break into better money was "to get those sons-of-bitches bidding against each other." In 1927 Joseph Shaw, as the new editor, lured Hammett back to *Black Mask* from advertising writing with a higher word-rate, at which time he began work on the novels which soon took him on to New York, Hollywood, and the really big money.

The massive domed building directly across Polk Street from Civic Center park is:

3 CITY HALL

I like to look at City Hall as a symbol of the law in 1920s San Francisco, since the old Hall of Justice of Hammett's day has long since been torn down. That building stood on Kearny Street opposite Portsmouth Square, where the gigantic Holiday Inn stands today. If you've seen any hard-boiled detective movies or read any hard-boiled detective books, you know that at some point the hard-boiled dick gets pulled into a bureaucrat's office where he gets to crack wise with the law. That happens in *The Maltese Falcon* when Sam Spade is called into the district attorney's office for questioning about the murders of his partner Miles Archer and the criminal Floyd Thursby. With the D.A. are an assistant district attorney and a male stenographer, who transcribes every word. The D.A. asks Spade to hazard a guess about the murders. Spade says, "My guess might be excellent, or it might be crummy, but Mrs. Spade didn't raise any children dippy enough to make guesses in front of a district attorney, an assistant district attorney, and a stenographer." Scribbling furiously, the stenographer tracks the rapid-fire dialogue which follows. Suddenly Spade pauses and asks him, "Getting this all right, son? Or am I going too fast for you?" Spade tells the D.A. if he wants to see him again to call Sid Wise, his lawyer, and slap a subpoena on him. Exit: Sam Spade.

Construction on this building was begun in 1913, and the dedication occurred in December of 1915. The *previous* City Hall near the corner of Grove and Hyde had taken twenty-nine years to build, and was occupied in 1899. During the 1906 earthquake it fell apart rapidly — the shoddy but incredibly expensive construction became a symbol of the graft which had dominated San Francisco's political scene for so many years. Stay alert while reading Hammett's San Francisco tales and you'll

find many references to the contemporary social and
political scene of the City.

*Head west around the north side of City Hall on
McAllister Street, past the statue of Hall McAllister after
whom the street is named. Cross Van Ness Avenue and go
another block west to the corner of McAllister and
Franklin. The building on the northeast corner is:*

4 580 MCALLISTER

In the "Whosis Kid," (1925) one in the series of twenty-
eight short stories about the gumshoe work of the
Continental Op, the jewel thief Inés Almad has an
apartment in this building, on a top floor in the rear, at the
east end. The number "580" is never mentioned in the
story, but there can be no doubt whatsoever that this
building, which was standing at the time, is the one where
the action takes place. The building is said to be at
Franklin, on the corner with McAllister, with the front
door opening on McAllister Street and the rear door
opening onto Redwood Street, an alley on the north side.
The description is so exact that the artist in New York in
the 1940s who drew the map for this story's appearance in
the Dell Mapback edition of *The Return of the
Continental Op* pointed an arrow right to this corner.

I suggested in my quick introductory biography of
Hammett that by 1934 he was the uncrowned king of the
crime story in America. The multimedia triumphs of the
comic strip *Secret Agent X-9*, the fast sales for his new
novel *The Thin Man*, and movie versions of both *The Thin
Man* and *Woman in the Dark* were not the only indicators.
When Knopf brought out the hardback of *The Thin Man*
that year, he used a photo of Hammett himself, posing
with a cane and hat as Nick Charles, for the cover.
Hammett was famous in his own right, and he was
earning respect. In 1934, *The Maltese Falcon* was
reprinted in Random House's Modern Library series, the
first contemporary detective novel so honored, joining

580 McAllister

titles by Hemingway and Faulkner and Joseph Conrad, and it went through several printings.

Hammett wrote a special introduction to the Modern Library reprint of the *Falcon*, and said that the Spade novel came about because "somewhere I had read of the peculiar rental agreement between Charles V and the Order of the Hospital of St. John of Jerusalem, that in a short story called 'The Whosis Kid' I failed to make the most of situation I liked, that in another called 'The Gutting of Couffignal' I had been equally unfortunate with an equally promising denouement, and that I thought I might have better luck with these two failures if I combined them with the Maltese lease in a longer story."

(The lease required the gift of one living falcon *each year* for Emperor Charles V of the Holy Roman Empire from the Knights Hospitalers, *as rent* for the one hundred twenty-two square miles of the island of Malta, located about sixty miles south of Sicily. Hammett, who had been paying $45 *a month* for furnished rooms in Eddy Street, obviously was impressed by this arrangement.)

The other Op tale he mentions, "The Gutting of Couffignal," takes place on a made-up island named Couffignal in San Pablo Bay north of San Francisco, most likely modeled on Tiburon and Belvedere. The short fat detective is stuck with the second-most boring assignment possible: guarding wedding presents. (The *most boring* assignment is the flip side of guarding wedding presents, a divorce case.) As the Op settles in for the night with his copy of *The Lord of the Sea*, a gang of crooks assaults the island. They blow up the one bridge leading to the mainland, then they begin to loot the place. They gut the bank and jewelry store as they storm over Couffignal, casually slaughtering people right and left. These crooks are so mean they even kill the butler and steal the wedding presents the Op has been guarding.

In the meantime, the Op has been hustling his short fat body all over the island, shooting it out with them and trying to figure out who is behind the plan. Tussling with a crook, he sprains an ankle. He limps around and by the time the Coast Guard finally arrives, he knows who the crooks are; he arranges for the entire gang, with the exception of one member, to be rounded up without further gunplay.

The mastermind of the gang is still at large. She's a beautiful, evil, Russian princess; the Op intends to nab her personally. He starts to hobble up to the house he knows she's in, but his sprained ankle won't carry his weight. He takes a crutch from a crippled newsboy, limps up to the house and confronts the woman. In another tussle, the crutch is knocked from his grasp. He falls back into a chair, hauling out his .38 special. She tries to bribe him. All the loot is in the basement: the two of them can become partners and get away with it yet! The Op tells her the simple facts: detecting is his job; it is the only job he knows; it is the only job he enjoys; you can't measure any amount of money against that. She says he can have anything he asks for. Coming from a beautiful evil Russian princess in a story written for a pulp magazine like *Black Mask*, in all probability she's not referring to home cooking. The Op thinks, nix on that — he doesn't know where these dames get their ideas, anyway.

The princess figures she can escape with her own skin, at least. The Op can't get up to run her down, and surely he wouldn't shoot a woman. She goes for the door. He shouts at her to stop. When she gets to the doorway, the Op pumps a bullet into her leg and she drops, staring at him in shock. He shouts at her: "You ought to have known I'd do it! Didn't I steal a crutch from a cripple?"

A clear case, as in *The Maltese Falcon*, of the beautiful, evil lady type figuring she's got enough oomph to get away with her plots, then finding out at the end that oomph is not enough.

In "The Whosis Kid" all the action occurs in San Francisco, including a shoot-out on the north sidewalk of McAllister just east of Inés Almad's apartment, car chases in the Haight and North Beach, and more. In this single Continental Op tale the main plot structure for *The Maltese Falcon* is quite evident. Inés Almad, the dapper Edouard Maurois, and a young homicidal maniac known as the Whosis Kid are partners in a jewel heist in Boston. They plan for Inés to take the jewels to Chicago while the two men stay on in Boston to establish alibis and let the heat cool off. Later the three will meet in Chicago, split the take three ways, and separate. But Inés makes a deal on the side with Maurois to meet him in New Orleans, ditching the Whosis Kid, for a two-way split. At the same time she works a triple cross. She tells the kid she'll meet *him* in St. Louis, and they'll divide the jewels up between them. Instead, she ditches them both and comes to San Francisco, where they track her down. If you recall the plot of the *Falcon*, Brigid O'Shaughnessy and Joel Cairo are supposed to steal a jewel-covered statue of a falcon for the fat man, but Brigid betrays both Cairo and Gutman and comes via Hong Kong to San Francisco, where they track her down. In the short story, the Continental Op gets stuck in the middle of the resulting action. In the novel, the thieves find they must deal with Sam Spade.

Another striking similarity between story and novel is that at the end of "The Whosis Kid," we find the principal characters all gathered here in Inés' apartment, waiting for her to reveal where she's got the jewels hidden — just as in *The Maltese Falcon* we find Spade, Brigid, Gutman, Cairo, and the young homicidal maniac of that work, Wilmer Cook, all waiting in Spade's rooms for his secretary to bring in the black bird the next morning.

When the jewels appear in the short story, guns blaze in 580 McAllister, and the Op faces a tense situation in a suddenly darkened, bullet-riddled apartment, with the Whosis Kid somewhere nearby with a gun ready, and Inés also lurking in the dark, with a knife.

Go around Inés' apartment house, up Franklin half a block, then duck right into Redwood alley, or what little remains of it since the State of California erected the large state office building which covers the rest of this block in the late 1980s. It is worth a look for a moment, for what I call the:

5   UNEXPECTED PALM TREE STOP

You can go past the front of this building a million times and never dream that there's this huge palm towering over the back courtyard. At one point in the story the Whosis Kid walks all the way down Redwood from Van Ness — more of the street was available for young homicidal maniacs to stalk down in the 1920s — then goes into the rear door of the court and into the building to search Inés' room for the jewels.

Of note is the cover story the Op comes up with to explain himself to Inés, as he tries to worm his way into the plot: he tells her he is a bootlegger. She says to him, "And you are the bootlegger?" "Not *the*," I corrected her; "just *a*. This is San Francisco."

Return to Franklin, take a right, then another right on Golden Gate. The next place for a brief stop is at Turk and Hyde a few blocks to the east. Here on the northwest corner of the intersection a small parking lot now does business where once stood:

6 408 TURK

As of this writing, 408 Turk is the only known Hammett residence in The City to have been razed. He kept a first floor room for a period in the early twenties; at the same time he and his wife had an apartment two blocks away in 620 Eddy. Remember that in 1921 Hammett was still an operative for Pinkerton at $105 a month, $45 of which went to rent the place on Eddy. In 1922 he began taking courses at the Munson vocational school, making his first sales to magazines late in the year. It's hard to see how he could have afforded a separate place for the purpose his daughter Mary Jane recalled. In the *City* interview she said her father "kept his India ink" in his room at 408 Turk, adding, "he used to do a lot of sketches." (Josephine Dolan Hammett reminded her daughter, "You were little, you know.") Today, it's hard to credit a recollection of "sketches" against the scenarios imagination draws forth: here was a place where Hammett could have all-night poker games with his pals, win enough cash to pay for this extra room and buy a little ground round, a place in which a Pinkerton op could meet underworld contacts without involving his wife and infant daughter. . . .

The apparent truth behind this separate place is far less exciting. When the tuberculosis slipped out of remission, Hammett was advised by doctors to limit contact with his family to avoid contaminating them. When the TB became active, the Veterans' Bureau paid for this room, because Hammett had picked up the disease while in the army. When he became seriously sick, they continued to give him varying amounts of disability pay. He kept this room away from Eddy Street, then, to avoid infecting Jose and Mary Jane with TB.

From this corner go west on Turk to Larkin, turn right one block, then left on Eddy. Less than halfway up the block on the north side you'll come to:

7 620 EDDY

The Crawford Apartments are a major Hammett site. Of the eight years in San Francisco, Hammett lived almost five of them in this building. Even if you factor in some months in 408 Turk and possibly some other TB-time apartment that is unknown today, this place remains his longest residence in The City.

620 Eddy

Soon after their marriage, on July 7, 1921, once they had decided to stay in San Francisco, he and his wife set up housekeeping here in a $45-a-month furnished apartment. It had living room, a small bedroom with a Murphy bed folding down out of the wall, a kitchen, and a bath. It was steam heated.

The Hammetts lived in this small apartment until early 1925, when Hammett sent his wife and daughter to live with Josephine's relatives in Montana for six months. Hammett suffered serious lung hemorrhages in this building. When his family returned they reunited here in 620 Eddy, but in a larger apartment.

It was here that Hammett began to write. Too sick to continue as a Pinkerton man, hoping to carve out a name for himself and also earn enough money to support his family, he sat down at this address and wrote roughly half of all the short fiction he would complete. He did not work on the novels in 620 Eddy. Those came later, but he composed most of his Op tales — "Arson Plus," "Zigzags of Treachery," "The Scorched Face" and many more — as well as occasional non-series tales, such as "The Crusader," which appeared in *The Smart Set* for August 1923 under the name of his infant daughter, Mary Jane Hammett.

In *City*, Jose Hammett said that he wrote directly on the typewriter, and went through draft after draft on a story until he got it to his satisfaction. In the first of the apartments, which was small, he placed the typewriter on the kitchen table. In the next, larger apartment, they set up a writing table for him in the living room. She said they got letters from *Black Mask* — maybe from the editorial staff, maybe from the readers, maybe from both — which demanded, *More action*! *More action*! She said that Hammett was "kind of upset about that," but then he apparently decided to give the Blackmasking public what it wanted.

The Continental Op shorts and novelettes in *Black Mask* today stand as hallmarks of pulp magazine violence, as Hammett put the fat sleuth through the meat grinder in story after story. If you wanted violence, these stories had it. An Op tale from 1923, the first year of the series, was titled — believe it or not, but it's true — "Bodies Piled Up." The first Hammett novel to make it into hardcover, the Op adventure *Red Harvest*, is a symphony of mayhem. Even the hard-boiled little detective reels under the number of deaths and realizes the urge to kill is making him "blood simple."

The Op tales offer more than mindless acts of violence, of course. The picture drawn of San Francisco and its environs alone is reason enough to seek out these stories. They also contain a wealth of background lore from Hammett's years with Pinkerton, and in a real sense perform as detective procedurals, showing the reader how it is done. In "Zigzags of Treachery," (1924) for example, Hammett *via* the Op explains the four cardinal rules of shadowing: 1) keep behind the suspect; 2) never attempt to hide; 3) act naturally, no matter what the situation; 4) never meet the suspect's eye.

With these tales by 1926 Hammett had set the stage for the revolution to come in crime fiction, and nailed down his claim as the father of the realistic detective story. Of course, "realism" is an imperfect term — it is hard to believe the overweight Op could have dodged all the bullets and knives Hammett has him dodge. But the presentation of a "tough" world was a realism appropriate for postwar America. It was a mood or an attitude people could understand, even if the violence taking place was *not* right down their own street.

The stories that poured out of 620 Eddy also clearly indicate that Hammett was having fun writing them, and was willing to play with formulas which most of the other fictioneers were taking seriously. His story "The Creeping Siamese" (1926) satirizes the stereotypes of sinister Asians which overpopulated the pulps, as a movie theater owner claims he has been robbed by a group of "creeping Siamese" and the Op states, "Being around movies all the time has poisoned his idea of what sounds plausible." In another novelette, "Corkscrew" (1925), Hammett moves the Op into a cowboy town in Arizona in a hilarious sendup of westerns. Some commentators just can't seem to believe that Hammett was having fun; in *Shadow Man* Richard Layman says of "Corkscrew" that "throughout, the story borders on parody." Hey, it *crosses the border*. It's one of the great fun reads that made Hammett such a draw for *Black Mask*.

Hammett's daughter Jo once said that she finds her father's most characteristic voice in the sardonic humor that enlivens the Op tales. One specific example she gave comes from the novelette "Dead Yellow Women," set in San Francisco's Chinatown, where Hammett sends up such characters as Fu Manchu in the figure of Chang Li Ching, and also parodies the typical mysterious Chinatown treatment by having the plot revolve around the politics of China versus Japan, instead of the usual yellow peril hokum. Chang makes fun of the Op almost every time they meet with his exaggerated titles for the detective: "The Emperor of Hawkshaws, the Father of Avengers, the Lord of Snares, the Disperser of Marauders, the King of Finders-Out, the Grand Duke of Manhunters." The Op thinks, "This old joker was spoofing me with . . . a burlesque of the well-known Chinese politeness," but finally he gets tired of the routine and begins to give it back. And here's the moment where Jo heard her father's voice in the words of the Op:

> "Not knowing who he was until too late, I
> beaned one of your servants last night. . . . I
> know there's nothing I can do to square
> myself for such a terrible act, but I hope
> you'll let me cut my throat and bleed to death
> in one of your garbage cans as a sort of
> apology."

Jose Hammett also said that during their years in this building Hammett tried other kinds of writing — his first ad copy apparently was a blurb he did for a shoe store in exchange for a pair of shoes. Needing more money than he was making from the pulp sales, he placed an ad in the paper asking for any kind of honest work and noted that he could write, and landed a job writing ad copy for Samuels Jewelers. In the 1926 City Directory Hammett listed himself at this address as "advertising manager of A.S. Samuels Co." and devoted most of his attention to that job. Only three stories saw print in *Black Mask* that year.

In 1926 the Hammetts would split up again for a few months, and when his wife and two daughters returned later in the year they reunited in 1309 Hyde Street.

Mrs. Hammett in the City *interview distinctly recalled that their landlady in 620 Eddy was a bootlegger. She said, "We used to peek down out the window and see all the cops coming and going." That was during Prohibition, of course, but in some ways things haven't changed that much. I thought it was appropriate, as I was standing with a tour group on a corner in the Tenderloin, that a crazed old guy denizen of the neighborhood stopped and shouted out, "Tell them! Tell them — they're all crack house! Crack houses!" In the twenties liquor was prohibited and Hammett's landlady was a bootlegger, today drugs are illegal but you can buy them on street corners all over town. The social reality is much the same.*

Return to Larkin and turn left. Pause mid-block where Willow alley enters Larkin and contemplate one of the ongoing puzzles about Hammett and his work:

THE PUZZLE OF THE CITY STREETS

In the Op story "Fly Paper" (1929) a woman dies from arsenic poisoning. A man and woman suspected of having knowledge of the crime are interviewed by the Op and another operative from the Continental Detective Agency in an apartment building in 601 Eddis Street. Yes, *Eddis*. Not Eddy half a block to the south or Ellis half a block to the north, but *Eddis Street*.

In the same issue of *City of San Francisco* magazine that ran the interview with Hammett's wife, Joe Gores has an article entitled "A Foggy Night," in which he tries to pinpoint all the buildings used in *The Maltese Falcon* and as many sites from Hammett's Op stories as possible. Gores is the author of several detective novels, including the series about Daniel Kearny and Associates of San Francisco. Like Hammett, Gores was an investigator before turning to writing, working a dozen years as a detective, nine of them with David Kikkert and Associates (which is to his Kearny series what Pinkerton is to the Continental Detective Agency). Gores says he became a detective out of his fascination with the Continental Op stories. His major connection to Hammett today is his 1975 novel, simply titled *Hammett*. The premise is that it is 1928 in San Francisco and Hammett has not worked for Pinkerton in something like six years — his manhunting skills have grown rusty. He is about ready to make his assault on New York and Hollywood and the really big money, but one of his friends is murdered and Hammett feels it necessary to put his gumshoes back on and solve one last case. During *his* years in San Francisco, Francis Coppola picked up an option on this novel, and in 1982 the film *Hammett* was released, produced by Coppola, directed by Wim Wenders, with Frederic Forrest starring as Dashiell Hammett.

Gores presents the problem of *Eddis* Street in his article: "Hammett freaks have argued for years whether this is meant to be 601 Eddy or 601 Ellis." He concludes that 601 Ellis Street was the address Hammett intended to be taken for 601 Eddis, saying "in neither Hammett's day nor our own was there ever a 601 Eddy." However, it clearly states in this story that the building overlooks Larkin Street. The 700 block of Ellis *begins* at Larkin; 601 Ellis overlooks Hyde a block back. The 600 block of Eddy, however, *does* begin at Larkin.

Many Hammett fans seem to feel that *every* building in every story was based on an actual place, that if just a *little* more description had been added you could find the building today, presuming it had not fallen before urban renewal. They have cause — the street descriptions in "The Whosis Kid" are precise enough for a cartographer, and much of *The Maltese Falcon* tempts in the same direction. In other stories, however, Hammett becomes very vague. In "The House in Turk Street" (1924) we know the Op is trapped in a single family house in a residential block of Turk, but no cross street is ever mentioned; it could be any house in a large number of blocks of Turk.

The puzzle of these city streets continues to bother Hammett's readers, though I don't know of any fistfights that have broken out between the various factions. For myself, I think Hammett sometimes went out and plotted the routes the Op follows on foot, or had good recall of a particular building when he needed it. In other cases I think he was trying to get the grocery money together and wrote, "there was a house on Turk Street." And that's all there was to it, no special house, no particular block. And when he described the scene at 601 *Eddis*, sitting at a typewriter at a desk which may have looked down into Willow, midway between Eddy and Ellis, I think he was *having fun* with the "*Black Mask* junk."

Other puzzles concerning Hammett will come up — but if you want a real puzzle, then ask yourself why would someone with TB settle in foggy San Francisco?

Continue up Larkin, across Ellis (drivers will have to loop around for a legal approach), until Olive Street opens at midblock. Turn into Olive and go down the alley. On the north side, slightly more than halfway through the block, stands a red brick building, easily spotted because of a huge vent pipe. Near the top of the wall, still discernable, is lettering for:

8 BLANCO'S

This was a restaurant where the Op ate a meal in the last Continental Op novel, *The Dain Curse*. Hammett dedicated this book to Albert S. Samuels, his employer at Samuels Jewelers, and placed about half the action in San Francisco, including the Op's run-in with a weird religious cult over on Van Ness Avenue. In some ways the novel's so timely it could have been written yesterday. But if you go around today to the front of this building on O'Farrell, you'll see that it no longer houses Blanco's but is home of The Great American Music Hall. You may have been at a concert, listening to the Bobs or David Grisman, not knowing you were in what was once a famous restaurant and Hammett site.

Blanco's in Olive Street

Hollywood simply was not interested in *The Dain Curse* during Hammett's lifetime, though it finally came to the TV screen in 1978 as a three part mini-series. The producers of this version had no faith in Hammett's vision of the Op as a short fat unmemorable sort of character, one who wishes to remain so deliberately unmemorable that when he talks about his casework he won't even give the reader his name. On TV, then, you did not find a short fat actor as the hero. James Coburn, looking more like Hammett himself than like the Op, played the part of detective *Hamilton Nash*. William F. Nolan once pointed out it *does* sound much like *Hammett*, *Dash*, as the makers of *The Dain Curse* try for a clear association between author and sleuth, as happened in *The Thin Man*. Personally, when I think of an actor for the part of the Op, I always picture Charles Durning — short, fat, great performer — to me the Op looks like Durning in the movie *The Sting* dressed in a hat and trenchcoat as he chases Robert Redford through a railroad yard. . . .

The people doing this TV adaptation clearly were unaware that the way had been opened long before to have an *unnamed* hero. This was done in the first successful film version of a Continental Op novel — a movie in many ways as pervasively influential through popular culture as is *The Maltese Falcon* starring Bogart, or the films of Nick and Nora Charles (which have led to a legion of husband-and-wife detecting teams in novels and television). In 1961, the year Hammett died, *Yojimbo* (or, *The Bodyguard*), directed by Akira Kurosawa, gives screenplay credit to Kurosawa and Ryuzo Kikushima, and is unmistakably a loose adaptation of *Red Harvest*. Kurosawa later said that *Yojimbo* was based on "an American detective story" (in one of the editions of his *Movies on TV*, Leonard Maltin gets author right but misidentifies *Yojimbo* as deriving from *The Glass Key*).

Watching the movie, you can see how well Kurosawa had studied the Hammett tales, in which the Op usually gives his age as late thirties to early forties, and never reveals his name. He will say, of course, something like "I told her my name" or "I told him my name was John Smith," but his real name remains unrevealed. Toshiro Mifune plays the wandering samurai who comes into a village torn by a war between two rival gangs, as Kurosawa simplifies Hammett's plot a bit — the town the Op comes into seethes with the struggle between several gangs *and* a crooked police force. When asked his name Mifune hesitates, scratches the stubble on his chin (borrowed not from Hammett but from Bogart, whose unshaven face became one of his trademarks in *The Treasure of the Sierra Madre*, *The African Queen*, et cetera). He walks across the room, looks out a window onto a field of mulberries, then says his name is "*Kuwabatake* (Mulberry Field) *Sanjuro* (Age Thirty). . . . going on forty, though." In the 1962 sequel, *Sanjuro*, the process is repeated: asked his name, Mifune rubs the bristle, says "My name is . . . ," looks around, sees flowers, "*Tsubaka* (Camellia) *Sanjuro*. But pretty soon I become *yonjuro*." Sanjuro — thirty-something; yonjuro — forty-something. Some of the dialog in *Yojimbo* evokes Hammett precisely, like the time a man says if you kill one or one hundred, "you only hang once"; one of the three short stories Hammett wrote about Sam Spade was titled "They Can Only Hang You Once."

In 1964 another version of *Red Harvest* appeared, not as a samurai movie but as a spaghetti western: *A Fistful of Dollars*, directed by Sergio Leone, and bringing an unshaven Clint Eastwood to the big screen in the role that would make him an international superstar: (pay attention) The Man Without a Name. Kurosawa protested the boosting of the *Yojimbo* plot, two rival gangs at war in a town and the lone gunfighter coming in and stirring up trouble, but Leone pointed out that the idea of a guy scurrying back and forth between two forces and creating havoc could be traced back to the mid-1700s in Italy and Carlo Goldoni's *commedia dell'arte* farce *Servant of Two Masters*. Yes, but it seems Hammett was the writer who brought the concept into the twentieth century and made it violent, as the Op tames that town modeled on Butte.

Leone went on to direct Eastwood in two sequels, *For a Few Dollars More* (1965) and *The Good, the Bad, and the Ugly* (1966). And I still can't see why, if Clint Eastwood can get through three movies without having a name, someone in Hollywood couldn't hire a short fat actor to star as a never-named Continental Op. It may happen yet, as various producers try to clear rights for a *direct* adaptation of *Red Harvest* for the screen. At one point, Bernardo Bertolucci had his eye on it as "an American Marxist opera."

Return to Larkin, turn left. The next site is on the south side of Geary between Larkin and Hyde:

9 811 GEARY

This apartment building is where the respected science fiction, fantasy, and supernatural horror writer Fritz Leiber lived for several years, from January, 1970, shortly after coming to San Francisco, until 1977, when he moved farther down Geary Street. During his first years in this building he happened to reread *The Maltese Falcon* and realized that he was living right on the edge of the action: "Geary Street between Hyde and Market is the spine of *The Maltese Falcon* — most of the action was on or near it, though once Spade uses the streetcar on Sutter." In *California Living*, the magazine supplement of the Sunday *Chronicle* for January 13, 1974, Leiber published "Stalking Sam Spade," the first article to survey sites used in the novel. He concluded that Spade lived in an apartment building near Geary and Hyde, because at one point Spade rides the 38 Geary streetcar from downtown, debarks at Hyde, and goes "up" to his rooms. "Up" stairs or an elevator, figured Leiber, though he did not say nor even secretly believe that Spade went up the stairs in 811 Geary where he himself was living.

In this same period, from late 1973 through 1975, Leiber also wrote a supernatural horror novel completely set in San Francisco, *Our Lady of Darkness*, published in 1977. The hero of that book, Franz Westen, also lives here in 811 Geary in 607; the description and view exactly matches Leiber's apartment, one floor down at 507. All action in this book occurs during two days in the mid-seventies, but Leiber throws in flashback sequences to earlier periods in San Francisco's history, drawing upon such literary figures as Ambrose Bierce, Jack London, and George Sterling. And in a scene from the twenties, Dashiell Hammett comes onstage as an actor in the narrative.

You may think it odd: Hammett, hard-boiled detective writer — what's *he* doing in a ghost story? Hammett had an interest though, because in 1931 his name appears as editor of the anthology of horror tales *Creeps by Night* from the John Day Company, which featured supernatural fiction by William Faulkner, John Collier, and other well-known authors of the time, and also offered early hardcover publication for the writers H. P. Lovecraft and Donald Wandrei, whose work had appeared in the pulps. Today researchers debate how much Hammett contributed as "editor," figuring an in-house editor may have done most of the selecting of stories for the book, but there is no doubt that Hammett wrote the appreciative introduction.

The next site is one block to the north on the corner of Post and Hyde. Whether you move on foot directly up Hyde or take your machine along Geary, up Larkin, and right down Post, you might notice that you are in one of the most authentically 1920s Hammett-era parts of The City. From the corner of Post and Hyde, in particular, the skyline looking to the north and to the south are very much the same skylines Hammett would have seen as he climbed this block from the 38 Geary stop or walked down the hill to pick up the streetcar. (I find it hard to believe, based on the traffic on the street today, but the 38 Geary streetcars ran both ways up and down Geary until about the mid-fifties.)

This entire area burned in the fire of 1906, of course, but many of the buildings in this neighborhood did not go up immediately after the cleanup — some of the ones you see were brand new or under construction when Hammett came to town in 1921. The four story brick building on the southeast corner of Post and Hyde was erected only four years before, in 1917, and had stood for only· a decade when Hammett took rooms in:

10 891 POST

With his wife and daughters living just seven blocks up Nob Hill in 1309 Hyde, Hammett moved here to the Charing Cross Apartments in 1927. The year before that, his TB had reactivated. His employer Albert Samuels gave Hammett a letter for the Veterans' Bureau that indicated he was too sick to hold a job, and they granted him 100% disability. Yet soon after he came to this address the TB was gone — and would never recur.

At this point Hammett had published about fifty stories or articles, and the new editor at *Black Mask*, Joseph T. Shaw, was enthusiastic about buying stories in longer lengths. For the February, 1927, issue Hammett provided the novelette "The Big Knockover," most likely written in Hyde Street. He followed it with a sequel, "$106,000 Blood Money," in the May issue, which was probably his first writing at this address. Hammett decided to go for

novel-length works, and these two comprise his first
novel, published as a separate book in 1943 under the title
Blood Money, and reprinted in paperback as *$106,000
Blood Money* and later as *The Big Knockover*.

The Big Knockover is Hammett's most lavish use of the
city of San Francisco. A gang of some one hundred
crooks storms into the Financial District, and robs two
banks which face each other across Montgomery at Pine.
The Op tears off after them through virtually every
neighborhood available to be shot up, including some —
such as Holly Circle — which are almost completely
unknown even to people who have lived in The City for
years. Hammett is having fun in this story, and in no
respect is it more apparent than in his tally of the crooks,
as the bodies pile up: "There was the Dis-and-Dat Kid,
who had crushed out of Leavenworth only two months

891 Post. Hammett lived in #401, top floor (left corner window)

before; Sheeny Holmes; Snohomish Shitey, supposed to
have died a hero in France in 1919; L. A. Slim, from
Denver . . . ; Old Pete Best, once a congressman . . . ;
Alphabet Shorty McCoy . . . ; Bull McGonickle, still pale
from fifteen years in Joliet; Toby the Lugs, Bull's
running-mate, who used to brag about picking President
Wilson's pocket in a Washington vaudeville theater . . . ;
The Shivering Kid . . . ; Happy Jim Hacker; Donkey
Marr, the last of the bow-legged Marrs, killers all, father
and five sons; Toots Salda, the strongest man in
crookdom, who had once picked up and run away with
two Savannah coppers to whom he was handcuffed. . . ."
If you want a three word argument on behalf of becoming
a fan of Hammett's writing, I'll give it to you: *The Big
Knockover.*

In his editorial notes on this story in *Black Mask*, Shaw
figured he had better cover the bets against charges of
exaggeration, so he pointed out that such a large-scale
robbery *was* possible, given the gang wars raging in
Chicago and that "the big mail truck holdup in Jersey
[had] found bandits using airplanes, bombs, and machine
guns — now Mr. Hammett pictures a daring action that is
stunning in its scope, yet can anyone be sure it isn't likely
to occur?" I guess Shaw didn't get out to movies much,
because I've long thought that Hammett pulled the idea
for *The Big Knockover* out of a 1920 silent feature
starring Lon Chaney called *The Penalty*. In this film
Chaney plays another of his famous grotesques, an
underworld king whose legs have been lost at the knees
because of the carelessness of a surgeon. His plans remain
big, though — Chaney is pulling hundreds of crooks into
town — and the town is San Francisco — in order to fight
off the police while he robs the Mint. Right there you
have the germ and more for Hammett's first novel. *The
Penalty* was filmed in part on location in San Francisco,
and features one spectacular dream sequence in which
Chaney imagines he once again has legs as he leads his
gang up the stairs of the Old Mint at Fifth and Mission
Streets.

Hammett followed *Knockover* with another Op
novelette, "The Main Death," and then sat down for
almost two years and began to produce novels. *Red
Harvest* opened in *Black Mask* in November, 1927, and

wrapped in February, 1928; *The Dain Curse* opened in November, 1928, and wrapped in February, 1929, just before Hammett left 891 Post for another apartment on Nob Hill. Incidentally, *The Dain Curse* supports the idea that Hammett actually had an interest in ghost stories. The atmosphere throughout evokes the idea of a supernatural curse hovering over the characters, and in one scene Hammett pictures the Op trapped by the religious cult and gassed — the fat man hallucinates that he is slugging it out with a ghost as he staggers toward a door.

And then Hammett began work on his next novel, one in which he abandoned the Continental Op, who was exhausted after two years nonstop shooting his way through three novels, and created a new detective. The name of the new detective was Sam Spade. The new novel: *The Maltese Falcon*, the most famous mystery ever placed in San Francisco, and a book that will hold its own against *any* other ever set here.

Hammett had told Ellery Queen that the Op was modeled on his Pinkerton supervisor in Baltimore, but of his new sleuth he said:

>   Spade had no original. He is a dream man
> in the sense that he is what most of the private
> detectives I worked with would like to have
> been and what quite a few of them in their
> cockier moments thought they approached.
> For your private detective does not — or did
> not ten years ago when he was my colleague
> — want to be an erudite solver of riddles in
> the Sherlock Holmes manner; he wants to be
> a hard and shifty fellow, able to take care of
> himself in any situation, able to get the best of
> anybody he comes in contact with, whether
> criminal, innocent by-stander or client.

Not only is 891 Post the building where Hammett created Sam Spade, it also is the building where Spade lives in the course of the novel. Fritz Leiber had figured that the detective lived in an apartment house near Geary and Hyde, because of that moment when Spade steps off the 38 Geary streetcar and goes "up" to his rooms. But Joe Gores points out a clue or two Leiber missed. At one point Spade is on the phone with Joel Cairo, and says, " . . . This is Spade. Can you come up

to my place — Post Street — now?" Later in the action
Spade goes out to see if Wilmer Cook, Gutman's boy
gunman, is still watching his apartment. The line reads:
"Post Street was empty when Spade issued into it."
Obviously, then, Spade lives on Post, and walked one
block *up* Hyde from Geary after leaving the streetcar.
Gores notes that correspondence between Hammett and
his publisher indicates that a draft of this novel existed
by early 1928, about midway through Hammett's stay
here — and what would be more natural, given the
existing clues, than that Hammett would place Spade's
apartment in the same building he himself lived in? Of
course, if you *really* want to quibble, you could say that
Spade lives in another twenties' vintage apartment
building in this area of Post, maybe one up the block,
but I think you'd have to be a sap to go for any address
other than 891 Post.

Tradition in this building has Hammett staying in 401
— top corner window overlooking Post, closest to
downtown. If we assume Spade *definitely* lived in
Hammett's own rooms, the evidence in the novel supports
the idea of a fourth floor apartment looking out on Post.
When Spade issues from the front door into the night to
look for Wilmer, he goes east a block (to Leavenworth),
crosses the street and walks west two blocks (to Larkin),
then returns to his building one block back (at Hyde). He
does not turn down into Hyde to check for Wilmer Cook
there, because anyone staking out 891 Post would have to
be on Post Street where he could see the front door, the
only easy entrance to the building. Since Spade from his
window notices Wilmer loitering in doorways a couple of
times, his apartment must have overlooked Post, not
Hyde.

We can be sure it's on the top floor because of an
incident toward the end of the novel, when Gutman offers
Spade $10,000 for the falcon — ten $1000 bills in an
envelope. Spade hands the envelope to Brigid to hold,
then gives it back to Gutman at his request; the fat man
palms a bill and reports it missing, with the apparent
intent of seeing how much Sam Spade actually trusts
Brigid O'Shaughnessy. Spade makes Brigid go into the
bathroom and remove her clothes, but before he searches
her he says to Gutman and Joel Cairo (at that moment

Wilmer Cook is unconscious on the couch): "The door will be open and I'll be facing it. Unless you want a three-story drop there's no way out of here except past the bathroom door." A three-story drop places Spade's apartment on the fourth and final floor.

It was in this apartment that Spade, at the end of *The Maltese Falcon*, set the edges of his teeth together and said to Brigid O'Shaughnessy: "I won't play the sap for you."

Start heading up Nob Hill for the next site near the corner of Clay and Hyde. If you're on foot and get tired and want to stop for a while, you might wish to consider during your break:

THE PUZZLE OF SPADE AND THE FALCON

When you think about it for a moment, Sam Spade is a damn fine name for a hard-boiled detective — and the puzzle is, where did Hammett come up with it? How? The "Sam" is obvious — Hammett's own first name; his wife and the people who knew him in his Pinkerton days all called him by Sam or Samuel. His co-workers at Samuels Jewelers, who read his stories under the name Dashiell Hammett, seem to be the folk who started calling him Dashiell. Then, in Hollywood, he became Dash. But Sam without Spade is not enough, that magic is not there; it's like Arthur Conan Doyle's initial name for his private consulting detective, Sherrinford Holmes — we can all be glad the name Sherlock came to his mind before the first story saw print.

In the September 22, 1980 issue of *New West*, Tim Hunter did a feature article on the making of the Coppola film *Hammett* — which went through a couple of directors, was over half-finished at one point and then reshot, and which ultimately had over thirty differing versions of the screenplay. Hunter notes that the screenwriters who worked on the project had very little overlap in their treatments, but that "there was one idea that just wouldn't quit: How did Hammett get the idea for Sam Spade's name?" One of the versions, Hunter writes, plays on the blond Satan image from the novel, with Hammett then saying "he's got my first name. But his last . . . it's like it came out of a grave . . . Spade. How's that, huh? A guy named Sam Spade?" Another treatment had Hammett punning after a shoeshine. Another had a takeoff on the expression "calling a spade a spade."

One of the most impressive explanations I ever heard was that Sam Spade was simply Hammett's name: Samuel Dashiell — the original name in French being *de Chiel*, which translates as the shovel or the spade. Sounds great, but the translation is wrong (I had it checked), with *de Chiel* at best sounding like *échelle*, the ladder.

And I have met a few people who claim Hammett got the idea from someone in their own families. One note I've kept from this guy named Spayde claims that his Aunt Estelle, Essie Spayde, worked for Pinkerton at the same time Hammett did, and that the family prided themselves on the fact that Hammett's famous detective was perhaps named after Aunt Essie. Yeah, sure, I've heard that one before.

And then there is the puzzle of the falcon — not the falcon from the novel, which seems to have been based on historic precedent. Hammett probably came up with the idea for the jewel-covered statue himself, but the idea of the living falcons given to Charles V has some substance, at least as much as the legends of Robin Hood, which persist. No, I'm puzzled about what happened to the falcon *from the Bogart movie*.

The most likely story I heard came from the actor Jackie Cooper, when I talked to him briefly at KGO radio as I was going out of a talk show and he was going in. As I recall, he said the statue was boosted from the prop room at Warners years ago by a guy who became, in time, an executive with one of the major TV networks. A nice guy, he allowed a cast to be made from which replicas of the bird could be marketed. Now, every detective agency in the country probably has a statue of the black bird discreetly displayed somewhere in the main office. Cooper said that Warners kind of wanted it back, but the guy is *not* going to give it back.

I also had a phone conversation once with man who was trying to track down the bird. He told me what he had heard: a few years after the Bogart film came out some guy in the Midwest wrote to Warners asking about the statue. The query ended up in the top offices, got passed to secretaries and then to go-fers, and finally ended up with the stock boy in the prop room, who rooted around for a while, located the statue, wrapped it and mailed it off to the guy. Later someone became curious about the statue, found the memos, realized the bird had been shipped out and quickly wrote to the fellow in the Midwest: *Where's the bird*?!

He wrote back: *What bird*?

As with the origin of the name Sam Spade, you may take the version you like best. But one thing I know, if I owned the original of the falcon from the Bogart movie, I'd be one nervous tour guide, because *that* bird has to be as coveted as the *rara avis* the Hospitalers intended for their emperor.

The next site is located on the west side of Hyde between Clay and Washington. After mentioning Bogart and the reference to Spade as "a blond Satan," how about a quick look toward the large brick building with the soaring awning on the southwest corner of Washington and Hyde? The Keystone Apartments , site of a big shoot-out in 48 Hours, *which introduced Eddie Murphy to the big screen. The scene filmed here featured Nick Nolte in a gun battle with a couple of bad-guy psycho-killers, played by James Remar and Sonny Landham.*

As with Charles Durning for the Op, I've long thought Nick Nolte is a perfect match for Hammett's description of Spade in The Maltese Falcon, *no offense to Bogart, who wasn't blond, large, slope-shouldered or Satan-faced, but who ran off with the role anyway. Also worth noting: the director of* 48 Hours, *Walter Hill, was at one point going to direct a film of* Red Harvest *from a screenplay he'd written; as a protege of Sam Peckinpah, Hill, I suspect, could do justice to the violence of the novel. But the place you came up the hill to see is:*

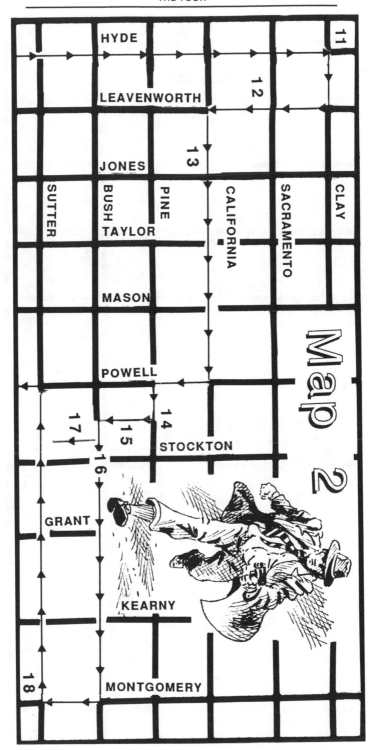

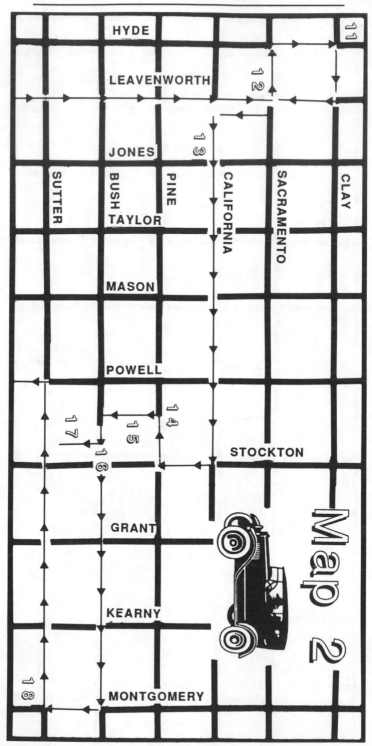

11 1309 HYDE

The Locarno Apartments: Hammett and his wife and daughters moved here late in 1926, after a separation of a few months. The first of their long separations came in 1925, when Hammett's TB flared up and he sent Jose to Montana to live with relatives for about six months. In 1926 the TB came out of remission again, and the Hammetts left 620 Eddy and moved into separate places: Hammett rented a room in 20 Monroe Street downtown while his wife took their two daughters and, for a change of pace, a break from city life, went to live on a farm in Marin County near what today is San Anselmo. When they reunited they came to this building overlooking the spur line for the California Street cable car.

Hammett apparently stayed with them here only for a brief time — a week, two weeks, a month — before

1309 Hyde

moving down the hill and renting a place for himself (and, later, Sam Spade) in 891 Post. He hiked up Hyde Street to see Jose and the girls, but after this time they would never again be together for long periods as a family as they had been in 620 Eddy. In the thirties and forties he saw them when he was in Hollywood, and spent the summer of 1950 with them; after coming out of prison in 1951, his health no longer allowed him to make the trip from the East Coast where he was living near Lillian Hellman, but his daughters, and the first of his grandchildren, visited him in the East.

Jose stayed in this apartment until late in 1928, when she moved to southern California. She made the move in part because she had a few relatives in the Los Angeles area, in part because she wanted to have the daughters near Hammett when he was in Hollywood. Obviously his ambitions were rapidly rising. His first novels had yet to appear in hardback from Knopf, but already he had his eye on the movies. His writing shows an interest in cinematic technique; he might have taken a theme from Henry James and *The Wings of the Dove*, but he wasn't adverse to copping from movies, like the major mob scenes he took from *The Penalty*, either. Hammett presented strong visual images, but his dialogue was even stronger. In *The Maltese Falcon*, especially the Bogart version, people mostly stand around in various rooms talking to each other, yet it's the dialogue that propels the story relentlessly forward. From one clue alone I think it safe to say that Hammett was strongly influenced by film, and intended his novels to end up in Hollywood: in the *Falcon* he actually gives Spade and Brigid O'Shaughnessy *a theme song*, played once on the phonograph when they are together and hummed later by Spade — "En Cuba."

The break with Jose occurred for a number of reasons, perhaps the largest being the change in expectations — she wanted a relatively normal home life but Hammett wanted to go Hollywood. In San Francisco Hammett began to drink heavily, and she had many problems with that. And while he was working for Samuels Jewelers, Hammett's attentions wandered to a woman named Peggy O'Toole, an artist in the ad department. In his introduction to the Modern Library reprint of *The Maltese*

Falcon Hammett wrote that he modeled Brigid O'Shaughnessy in part on this woman, and also on a woman who came into the Pinkerton office in San Francisco and hired Hammett as an operative to fire her housekeeper — she just couldn't do it herself.

When he came to dedicate *The Maltese Falcon* in 1930, the artist was history and the book was presented "For Jose."

Head east on Clay a block, turn south down Leavenworth a block to where it intersects Sacramento. The building on the southwest corner is:

12 1155 LEAVENWORTH

The San Loretto Apartments were Hammett's final stop in San Francisco. He moved here in March, 1929, from 891 Post, and by fall had left here for New York in company with a new lover, Nell Martin, who also had ambitions as a writer and would produce several novels; *Lovers Should Marry* (1933) she dedicated to Hammett. He dedicated to her the novel he was writing while they were together in this building and when they first reached New York: *The Glass Key*.

Tradition places Hammett in apartment 2 in this building, a studio bedroom with a small kitchen and bath, and in those days a Murphy bed folding out of the wall. The first floor windows look out over Leavenworth at the south end of the building. If the tradition handed down from manager to manager is correct, then 2 was his quarters when Hammett finished writing *The Maltese Falcon* in 1929, and where he revised the five-part *Black Mask* version for Knopf.

At this address Hammett listed himself for the first time in the City Directory as "writer," even though for almost seven years he'd written professionally. But he knew now he had made it — he was no longer living in the Tenderloin, he was on Nob Hill, about ready to leave for New York, and from there, for Hollywood. Many people

1155 Leavenworth

did not consider writing for pulps to be "real writing," but in 1929, Knopf would bring his first novels into hardcover — haul out two books from Knopf and the argument about whether or not he was a "real" writer would be over for most people. (I did have, however, a woman on the tour once who asked me towards the end of the walk, "But didn't Hammett ever try to write any *real* books?" I said, "Well, no, he only managed to write stuff like *The Maltese Falcon* — though you've got to consider that 95% of the 'real books' of Hammett's day haven't been read in fifty years." But she didn't get the point.)

Occasionally people get a little soft in the head and suggest Hammett had some romantic attachment to his days in San Francisco. The facts of the matter are: 1) after he got to Hollywood, Hammett could have afforded to live anywhere on earth he wanted to live; 2) he never came back to San Francisco to live, and returned only a handful of times on casual visits, having his chauffeur bring him up by limo. In the autobiographical fragment

Tulip, his days in San Francisco get no more attention than his days on Kiska or his time spent as a lunger in Tacoma or in Camp Kearny near San Diego. San Francisco was just another place he lived, and because he typically wrote about what he knew, he ended up setting most of his stories here, since he was in residence at the time he wrote them.

Looking at the matter today, it would be difficult to say how large, if intangible, a part of Hammett's appeal lies in the fact that Sam Spade *is* stalking over the hills of *San Francisco* through the winter night-fog in his hunt for the black bird. And while I think Hammett had enough talent to bring it off, I suspect I wouldn't enjoy *The Big Knockover* quite as much if it were set in Dubuque, Iowa. Personally, I doubt that Hammett thought of San Francisco much after he left this apartment. The only date I would bet money on The City coming to his mind — it would have been hard to miss the news — would have been on his forty-third birthday, May 27, 1937, the day the ribbon was cut on the Golden Gate Bridge.

The next site is only two blocks away, the tall building on the southwest corner of California and Jones:

13 1201 CALIFORNIA

About the only "big claim" I ever made for the Dashiell Hammett Tour is that if you survived the climb over Nob Hill and got to the end, you would have seen every single place Hammett is known to have lived in San Francisco. But if a residence someday is discovered near Ocean Beach or at Army and Dolores, hey, I'm not walking out to it. I was talking with Joe Gores once, and he told me the "big claim" he made, the discovery he was most proud of: he figured he was the person to locate three definitive sites from *The Maltese Falcon* — Sam Spade's apartment, Sam Spade's office building, and the apartment building the Coronet, where Brigid O'Shaughnessy stays through most of the novel. In the case of Spade's apartment and office, I completely agree with him. I think Gores nailed them down tight. In the case of Brigid's place, though, well, I have read his argument many times as he tracks Spade's movements to the Coronet, and I always fall off the cable car somewhere before he ends up in front of 1201 California.

1201 California

The Coronet in the novel *is* on California, to be sure, and if you're willing to accept Gores' choice, then stand in front of this building and look at the "C" emblazoned on the awning. That "C" stands for the Cathedral Apartments, but Gores suggests you think of it as standing for the Coronet, the place where Brigid summons Sam Spade soon after the murders of Miles Archer and Floyd Thursby. She has told Spade that her name is "Miss Wonderly," though registered here under the name "Leblanc." When he arrives, she tells him that her name really is Brigid O'Shaughnessy — she doesn't have a kid sister who is in trouble, she's in trouble herself. She says: "Help me. I've no right to ask you to help me blindly, but I do ask you. Be generous, Mr. Spade. You can help me. Help me." Spade looks her over and replies: "You won't need much of anybody's help. You're good. You're very good."

Another reason Gores opts for 1201 California as model for the Coronet is that in Hammett's first version of The Thin Man *(an unfinished fragment he set in San Francisco, which features not Nick and Nora but a Sam Spade-like detective named John Guild) the Cathedral Apartments are mentioned by name, proving Hammett was familiar with the building. I lean in the other direction, figuring it far less likely that Hammett would have used the same structure as an incidental site twice. Even in the Op shorts, Hammett seldom repeats anything but the standards such as the Hall of Justice.*

In this early version of The Thin Man — *published in* City *with the other features on Hammett* — *he also uses 1309 Hyde for a scene and places another in 1157 Leavenworth, one (nonexistent) number over from his last address in The City. Hammett seems to have started this novel in New York soon after wrapping* The Glass Key, *only to abandon it when he went to Hollywood. By 1933 he was so out of touch with the mood and the scene that he switched the action to New York and dropped John Guild in favor of Nick "It's too early for breakfast, I think I'll have a drink" Charles.*

As you cross Nob Hill, passing the old James Flood mansion, the Fairmont, the Mark Hopkins en route to the next sites on another shoulder of the hill, consider this big problem argued among Hammett fans:

THE PUZZLE OF THE BLOCKED WRITER

That fragment of the first try at *The Thin Man* may be seen today as a warning shot. In barely more than three years Hammett had written *The Big Knockover*, *Red Harvest*, *The Dain Curse*, *The Maltese Falcon*, and *The Glass Key*, but then he got his chance at Hollywood money and put the novel aside. Only when he was broke in 1933 did he manage to produce *Woman in the Dark*, a very short novel, if you're willing to consider it as a full-scale novel, followed by a new version of *The Thin Man*. Then, nothing more — not one finished short story, and only mere pages of the mainstream novels he started to write. The screenplay for *Watch on the Rhine* in 1942 marks the major rally of Hammett's later career, and then he was adapting a pre-existing work.

In 1934 Hammett as a novelist hit a solid wall of writer's block. The contributing factors seem clear enough today. For one thing, he was drinking as much as his alter ego Nick Charles, and in his case, the liquor may have dropped him. He no longer really *needed* to write anything after 1934 but quick stories for the screen and such high concept ideas as *The Fat Man*. If Hammett had not become so successful he would have had less money for partying and may have found it necessary to produce more books just to pay his way. And an equally large factor is that he divorced himself in the projected novels from his natural material, the crime story; staring at the blank sheets, he discovered that without an element of crime, Hammett novels just did not exist.

As years passed and people began to ask him about new books, Hammett would usually refer to the speed of composition — those five novels in three years, the last third of *The Glass Key* in one thirty-hour session, *The Thin Man* in two weeks. When he was being glib, he suggested that any writer who had that much control over style simply had nothing else to say. When he was being straightforward, he said he thought he would be able to do it again, just get away with Lillian Hellman to an island retreat or a farm for a month, maybe two months, to knock out a new book. But he could never do it again.

One part of the Nick and Nora *Thin Man* is hotly argued for what it may mean, what it suggests about Hammett's state of mind at the time he was pounding out the book. The section is in chapter 13 where he quotes some 1500 words on the subject of Alfred G. Packer, who in 1874 killed five companions in Colorado and cannibalized them: it's an exact quote taken from *Celebrated Criminal Cases of America* by Thomas S. Duke, published by the James H. Barry Company in San Francisco in 1910. Readers familiar with Hammett will recall that the only book Sam Spade had in his apartment was a copy of *Duke's Celebrated Criminal Cases*, and it seems Hammett kept a copy with him as he traveled.

Jerome Weidman once mentioned a time when he and Hammett were out walking, and he asked Hammett what the section with Packer *meant*, in terms of the symbolism of the novel. Hammett told him that an in-house editor for the novel had asked him for 1500 words more than he turned in, so he added the pages about Packer from *Duke's*. Weidman said he did not believe him — *surely* there was more to it than that — but he could not pull any more information out of Hammett. In support of Weidman's belief in the importance of the quote is an inscription Hammett wrote in a copy of *The Thin Man*, dated June 11, 1934: "For George H. Burr — with earnest assurances that it's all art. *Dashiell Hammett*." This copy shows up in rare book catalogs these days priced at more than $8,000 — (yes, about as much as Warners paid for all movie rights to *The Maltese Falcon*, for a single copy of an inscribed Hammett novel.)

So, the puzzle of the blocked writer boils down to this: does the use of the Packer incident from *Duke's* mean any of the things the critics suggest it does when they chew over Hammett's novels? Or, after blasting through *The Thin Man* in a couple of weeks, was Hammett so tired of it that he found it easier to lift 1500 words from a book at hand so he could get back to drinking?

Wind your way over the crest of Nob Hill and down in the direction of Union Square to Pine Street between Stockton and Powell. The Op sees some action a few blocks over between Leavenworth and Jones in the story "Death on Pine Street," also published under the title "Women, Politics and Murder" (1924). But to continue with the tour turn into the alley that opens on the south side of the 700 block of Pine:

14 DASHIELL HAMMETT STREET

Although he only managed to write mysteries and not "real books," Hammett made the cut when the names for streets were being handed out. The names did not come easily. Lawrence Ferlinghetti, the poet and cofounder of City Lights Bookstore, had the idea in mind for several years before he managed to get some action, and his first list of twenty names got trimmed to a dozen. Ferlinghetti had lived in Paris for some time, and liked the manner in which the French honored their writers and artists by naming streets after them — Avenue Victor Hugo, for example. (Someone told me recently that they even have a Housman Street in Paris named after A. E. Housman). So Ferlinghetti nurtured the idea that maybe a street such as Bush — not really a catchy name — might be renamed in honor of Mark Twain or Jack Kerouac. The major

The new Dashiell Hammett Street, 1989

obstacle to that plan is the length of the street, with lots of people who-can-spell-Bush-when-they-send-off-a-bill-but-might-have-trouble-with-Kerouac living along the way, and street signs for Public Works to change on every corner for miles. Too high a hurdle. However, take a street that is only a block long, with a minimum of residents to feel the impact of an exotic literary name, and you have a chance. On January 25, 1988, the San Francisco Board of Supervisors approved the proposal to rename several of The City's streets after writers and artists. On October 2, 1988 the names of those who received the honors were announced at a ceremony held in City Lights: Mark Twain, Jack London, Frank Norris, Richard Henry Dana, Isadora Duncan, Benny Bufano, Bob Kaufman, Ambrose Bierce, Jack Kerouac, Kenneth Rexroth, William Saroyan and Dashiell Hammett — and soon after that Public Works had up all the new street signs.

20 Monroe

Halfway down Dashiell Hammett Street on the east side you'll come to a building in which Hammett lived in those historic times when this block was named Monroe:

15 20 MONROE

Today 20 Dashiell Hammett Street, this is the place where Hammett rented a room when he and his wife left 620 Eddy Street in 1926. He was writing ad copy for Samuels Jewelers at this time, though in July he would have a serious recurrence of TB, and would be found lying unconscious on the floor of the advertising department in a pool of blood coughed out of his lungs. Two months later Samuels gave him a letter for the Veterans' Bureau, which allowed him to get 100% disability benefits.

In 1926 only three Op tales appeared in *Black Mask* in the January, February, and March issues, but Hammett placed an article on ad writing, "The Advertisement IS Literature," in *Western Advertising* in October. In 1927 he would begin his book reviews for *The Saturday Review of Literature*, do an occasional piece about ad writing, and in his new rooms in 891 Post Street start work on the novels.

During this time Jose took the two girls to live in Marin County, a decade before the new bridge would span the gate. When Hammett visited them, he took a ferry across the icy waters. They reunited in San Francisco late in 1926 in 1309 Hyde Street.

Despite the fact that it seems Hammett did not work on any of his fiction while residing in Hammett née Monroe Street, this address fascinates hard-boiled fans because of its tantalizingly close proximity to what today is the most famous Hammett site in San Francisco. Turn left out of Hammett onto Bush. Just half a block down to the right, you'll see where two flights of stairs emerge at the top of the:

Above the tunnel

16 STOCKTON TUNNEL

At 2 a.m. the telephone awakened Spade in his apartment in 891 Post. He said, "Hello. . . . Yes, speaking. . . . Dead? . . . Yes. . . . Fifteen minutes. Thanks." He dressed, phoned the Yellow Cab Company for a taxi, and had it drop him "where Bush Street roofed Stockton before slipping downhill to Chinatown." Then, "Spade crossed the sidewalk between iron-railed hatchways that opened above bare ugly stairs" — still a perfect description to this day — "went up to the parapet, and, resting his hands on the damp coping, looked down into Stockton Street."

Spade looked over toward a vacant lot on the west side of Stockton Street, where the north wing of the tall McAlpin apartments stands today, a white building smoked gray by exhaust fumes. To break the McAlpin down visually, notice that it has five bay window projections fronting on Stockton: the section of the building with the two lines of bay windows closest to Union Square was standing in 1928 when *The Maltese Falcon* takes place; the three lines of bay windows closer to the tunnel are part of the newer north wing, not yet built as Sam Spade stared through the fog at the billboard that fenced the lot away from the sidewalk on Stockton. He noted three men looking around the billboard at something in the lot, and saw flashlight beams playing over the dirt of the steep slope and the side of the McAlpin apartments halfway down the block.

And then Spade left the parapet and walked through the night-fog a short distance west on Bush to where a small group of men stood looking into:

17 BURRITT STREET

Beneath the street sign a bronze plaque tells all, summing up in one sentence why this alley is the most sought after Hammett landmark San Francisco: "On approximately this spot Miles Archer, partner of Sam Spade, was done in by Brigid O'Shaughnessy." The first murder in *The Maltese Falcon*! The crime that led to other deaths, and put Sam Spade on the trail of a time-lost statue of a mysterious black bird. A *classic* site for any hard-boiled literary hiker.

Attempts to put up a plaque began in the early sixties. Humphrey Bogart had died from cancer of the throat January 14, 1957, and Hammett died from cancer of the lungs January 10, 1961. Hammett-Spade-Bogey fans in San Francisco suddenly realized that in a sense Sam Spade was dead, and The City should do something to commemorate its most famous detective. People talked about putting up a marker, naming a street, *something*, yet nothing happened until the late sixties when the famous advertising man Howard Gossage heard about the idea.

Burritt

He got together with Warren Hinckle, journalist, a founder of *Ramparts* magazine. They worded the plaque, ordered it — but before it could be installed, Gossage died. Hinckle, writing, editing magazines, seems to have put the plaque in his house and forgotten about it for some five years. Until one night, late in 1973, an anonymous literary historian (and it wasn't me — I wasn't here in 1973) spray-painted the words "Miles Archer Was Shot Here" on the sidewalk in front of the Bush Gardens Japanese Restaurant, located on the northeast corner of Bush and Stockton, where the entrance to the Juliana

Hotel is today. The man running the restaurant didn't know what the words signified, and was intending to have them painted over, when some mystery fan told him what they meant. He figured, okay then, let them stay. Herb Caen gave the incident a big writeup in his column in the *Chronicle*. The daring commando action brought some publicity to the need for a plaque. Completely independent of that, Fritz Leiber was working up his "Stalking Sam Spade" article; in the Sunday paper, January 13, 1974, he wrote, "A few years ago some *Falcon* fans tried to get permission to put up a brass plaque in Burritt reading 'Here Brigid O'Shaughnessy shot Miles Archer.' The permission didn't come through, but it's still a nice idea."

With the mentions in the press, Hinckle's memory was jogged. *Wait a minute, somewhere around here!* . . . He brought out the plaque, the red tape was cut, and the plaque was installed on the Burritt side of the Matabelle Apartments on Tuesday, February 12, 1974, by James Kennedy, the owner of the building; by Marino Nibbi, a contractor; and by hard-boiled City Supervisor Quentin Kopp, more recently a hard-boiled State Senator.

Today the street sign reads "Burritt" in black letters on white, but Sam Spade came up to "a uniformed policeman chewing gum under an enameled sign that said *Burritt St.* in white against dark blue." The detective walked halfway down the alley to meet Tom Polhaus of the homicide squad. On the left, where the poured concrete section of the white apartment building is today, a board fence ran along the alley. Past it "dark ground fell away steeply to the billboard on Stockton Street below."

Fifteen feet down the hill Miles Archer's corpse lay, lodged between a boulder and the slope of the fog-damp earth.

The great interest in Hammett's brief stay in 20 Monroe for people today is the certain realization that walking between his room and his job for Samuels at 895 Market, Hammett would have gone past the future murder scene. Some days he may have hiked the half block west over to Powell Street and boarded a cable car down to the turntable, then cut across to the jewelry store on the southeast corner of Fifth and Market. But at other times he would have gone to the east, down the stairs at the tunnel, walked past the billboard and the lot it screened from the street — or come back that route in the evening after he and his co-workers had wrapped up their drinking session in John's Grill for the night, when the loneliness of the scene in the midst of the city would have been noted, even if he had stopped writing the Black Mask *junk, and as far as he knew at that moment, would never have need for another murder site again. Or, perhaps the tunnel, echoing like a cavernous machine shop with the passage of the Stockton streetcars, the stairs and the billboard meant more to Hammett than a likely place to bump off a sap like Archer who'd trust his red-headed client enough to follow her "up a blind alley with his gun tucked away on his hip and his overcoat buttoned." I sometimes suspect so, and imagine:*

THE PUZZLE OF THE BILLBOARD AND THE BRICK

When he wrote his introduction to the Modern Library reprint of *The Maltese Falcon*, Hammett singled out "The Whosis Kid" and "The Gutting of Couffignal" as two Op tales in which he had "failed to make the most of a situation I liked," but they were not the only Op shorts from which he lifted elements to rework in the novel about Sam Spade. In his first book about the father of the hard-boiled detective tale, *Dashiell Hammett: A Casebook* (1969), William F. Nolan points out that in "The House in Turk Street" (1924) the Op is alone in a room with the bad guys (a fat man, a femme fatale, a gunman) negotiating for his life, a preview of the final movement in the *Falcon* where Spade and the others wait in his apartment for the statue and try to figure out who'll be given over as "the fall guy" for the police. Nolan also targets the story "Who Killed Bob Teal?," published later in 1924; after reading this story, it is baffling that Hammett neglected to mention it with the others. Bob Teal, one of the regular operatives for the Continental Agency, who appears in several of the stories, is lured behind a billboard *by their client*, and killed. Joe Gores points out that Teal's murder scene was "behind a row of wooden signboards on the northeast corner of Hyde and Eddy — it was a vacant lot at the time." No question but that Hammett kept his eye out for vacant lots and that he did not like to use the same location twice — he needed a *fresh* billboard-screened lot for Archer's demise, and had one along that old route he had walked to Monroe. Or did that *route* mean more to him?

Jose and Mary Jane Hammett mention a low point in Hammett's career as a shadow man for Pinkerton. His wife said, "Another time he was shadowing someone but what he didn't know was that he was not shadowing one, he was shadowing two and the second one came up behind him and dropped a brick on his head." His daughter said, "You could feel it in later years. There was a dent in the back of his head like the corner of a brick."

The billboard on Stockton, circa 1928

(In her memoirs Lillian Hellman also mentioned "bad cuts on his legs and the indentation in his head from being scrappy with criminals" — the former coming from a fight during World War I when the Pinkertons burst into a house after a bunch of blacks who had stolen some dynamite. In the ensuing fracas Hammett was unaware for a few moments that one of the gang was lying on the floor with a knife, carving up his legs.)

When he recounted the brick episode in *Shadow Man*, Richard Layman put it this way: "Hammett was led by his suspect into an alley where the partner slammed him over the head with a brick." But Jose Hammett did not mention an alley. And she said the brick was *dropped* on his head. To leave the dent described by his daughter and Lillian Hellman, a free falling brick seems more likely than a brick swung by hand. *And* if Miles Archer had "too many years' experience as a detective to be caught like that by a man he was shadowing," I very much doubt that Hammett in his last year with Pinkerton would have followed his man into an alley. Miles only walked down Burritt because Brigid O'Shaughnessy was there, *his client*, whose sexual lure was like the call of the Lorelei. *And* then the issue comes up of *where* in San Francisco in the twenties — or today — could a crook spot the guy shadowing his partner, trail along, improvise a bit when he spotted some bricks, and get *into a position to drop a brick on the shadow's head*? It's lucky for Hammett that in the twenties everyone wore a hat, because a brick dropped on an unhatted head as it went down the stairs to the Stockton tunnel, or let go off the coping on top, could kill a guy.

What I wonder is this: Did Hammett, in 1928 when he had Miles Archer's corpse roll down the dirt hill behind the billboard, have in mind that time in 1921 when he himself had been played for a sap? And was the place where Hammett was dropped by the brick on the *other side* of that billboard, across from the spot where Sam Spade's partner got his?

The next stop on the tour is four blocks away from where Bush roofs Stockton, on the southwest corner of Sutter and Montgomery:

Hunter-Dulin Building (detail)

18 111 SUTTER

The Hunter-Dulin Building is the place tagged by Joe Gores as the office building of Sam Spade and Miles Archer in *The Maltese Falcon*. A casual reading of the novel easily spots the office in this vicinity, and some people have argued that Spade worked out of the impressive glass-fronted Hallidie Building across the way at 130 Sutter. Gores' argument in favor of 111 Sutter is painstaking and matches the street directions given in the novel perfectly — the clincher being the moment when Spade slips from his office "by way of an alley and a narrow court" over to Post and Kearny, where he flags a cab. Gores points out that the alley is Lick Place, and the only building that fits Spade's route at that moment and before is the Hunter-Dulin. He has me convinced. I think Gores is completely on the mark.

Of course, the Hunter-Dulin is much larger and more opulent than I ever imagined Spade's office building to be, but a lot of that negative expectation comes from Hollywood and the film noir of the forties and fifties,

111 Sutter

where it seems the detective usually keeps an office someplace in a run-down warehouse district. The grainy black-and-white film of the period reinforces this visual patterning. But in 1928 when *The Maltese Falcon* takes place you had a shortage of run-down warehouse districts downtown for a sleuth to rent offices in. With the exception of a very few buildings, San Francisco had burned to the ground twenty-two years before, from the waterfront west to Van Ness and south to Market, and in some areas beyond. This part of town was almost brand new — the Hunter-Dulin itself dates from 1926.

In any case, Sam Spade wasn't the kind of detective who would work out of a decaying warehouse; he wasn't a romantic sap like Chandler's detective Philip Marlowe, who would get offended by his clients' lack of ethics, return their retainer fee, and go on to solve the case for free. Spade today would match up with any yuppie lawyer on the make; he had an office in a big building because he wanted to draw in clients with money. He didn't short-change himself whenever money passed from hand to hand, and he only handed over the $1000 bill he had taken from Gutman to the cops because he knew that it, and someone to give them as the murderer, would let them close the casefiles on Archer and Thursby, and put him in the clear. He talked tough to the D.A., but he knew he wouldn't be able to pull anything out of the deal without giving *someone* to the D.A., even if if was Brigid, even if he *did* love her. He told Gutman that he'd *have* to deal with Sam Spade, like it or not, because San Francisco was *his* burg, but he had only been in The City about a year. Spade tells Brigid: "In 1927, I was with one of the big detective agencies in Seattle;" there is no doubt that his run-in with her and the fat man occurs in December, 1928. Yes, he talked tough, he had his lawyer ready, yet the only other case that comes his way the week the Maltese falcon is due to arrive in town is a penny-ante case of employee pilfering of the cash receipts at a small movie theater. In *The Maltese Falcon* Spade is the "hard and shifty fellow" Hammett said he was, but I don't think he was quite "a dream man" — that interpretation on the author's part probably owes more to the fact that in 1932 he sold three high-pay Sam Spade short stories to the slicks, in which Spade just waltzes through the mysteries. Spade, in the novel begun in 1928, skates right up to the edge, and the fact that he doesn't go over is no proof that he came out of the case unbloodied.

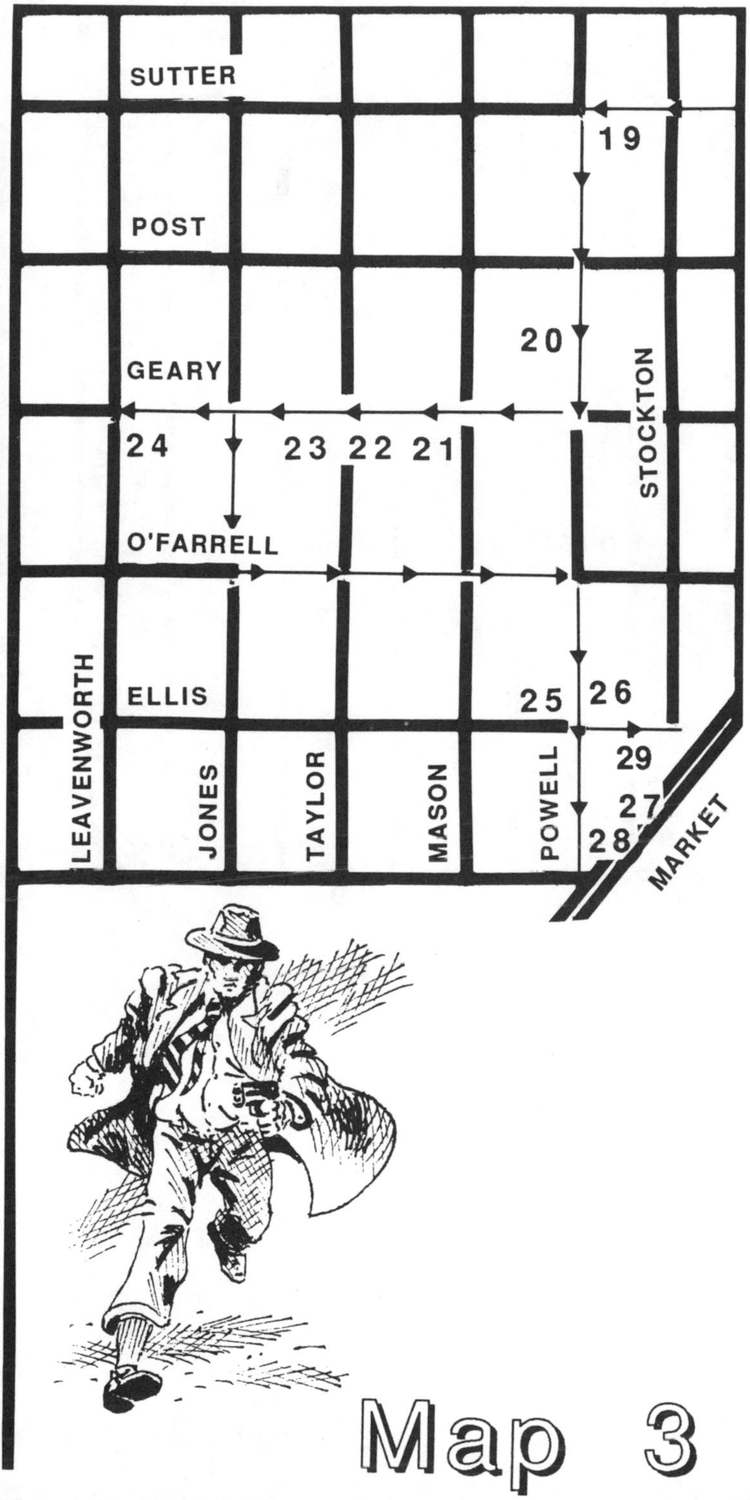

Map 3

SUTTER

19

POST

20

GEARY

24   23 22 21

STOCKTON

O'FARRELL

ELLIS

25 26

29

27

28

LEAVENWORTH

JONES

TAYLOR

MASON

POWELL

MARKET

Map 3

Before heading west up Sutter, make sure you check out the bird motifs on 111 Sutter. Since Hammett clearly went to some effort to accurately describe Spade's movements to and from this particular building, I wonder if, in his search for an office building that would "fit" a detective like Samuel Spade in the novel he had in mind, it wasn't the bird emblems that made him settle on the Hunter-Dulin? Again, an unknown. Another unknown is what happens between Spade and Iva Archer at the end of the novel. Mrs. Spade's son has been having an affair with his partner's wife, of course, though he has grown tired of her.

One of the crueler rumors circulated among inner circles of hard-boiled fans is that Ross MacDonald's detective Lew Archer is not Miles' issue, but Iva's illegitimate son Spade fathers. Ross MacDonald said he took his sleuth's name from Miles Archer — but who would name his detective after a loser like Miles Archer and not expect a little ridicule?

As you cross Kearny on Sutter, keep in mind that Sid Wise, of Wise, Merican, and Wise, Spade's lawyer, had his office in room 827 of a corner building at this intersection, corner unspecified. The next stop is on the southeast corner of Sutter and Powell:

19 SIR FRANCIS DRAKE HOTEL

In "Stalking Sam Spade" Fritz Leiber writes, "Caspar Gutman and Wilmer Cook are staying at the Alexandria on Geary." But Joe Gores selects the Drake here as his first choice for the fat man's hotel. Catch that "first choice." His follow-up selection *is* on Geary, the Clift. Obviously, we have some problems here, not the least of which is that no Alexandria Hotel existed in San Francisco. If it makes sense in terms of the way Hammett describes it, then it has to be based on an actual hotel.

The indication that it may be on Sutter comes during the scene where Wilmer Cook, the fat man's gunsel, meets Spade outside the detective's office building. Cook has guns in both pockets of his coat. He tells Spade

Gutman wants to see him. It is only a short walk up Sutter to the Alexandria — that would be the four blocks you just traveled from 111 Sutter to the Drake. They ride an elevator to the twelfth floor — the building has to be twelve stories high or higher. As they go down the hallway Spade slips behind Wilmer, tackles him and takes his guns. When they enter Gutman's suite, Spade quips: "A crippled newsie took them away from him, but I made him give them back." (A line indicating the novel's origins in the Op story "The Gutting of Couffignal," which featured Hammett's very best crippled newsboy scene.)

But when Spade first went into Gutman's suite earlier in the book, it says: "Doors in three of the room's walls were shut. The fourth wall, behind Spade, was pierced by two windows looking out over Geary Street." To go with the Drake, you have to presume that Hammett is describing a view out past Post Street and over Union Square. But he did not tend to be so loose with his words that he'd skip over a street or the park, which would have to be visible in this scenario. And then too, you have another possible contender in the Plaza, located at that time where the Grand Hyatt on Union Square is today, Stockton between Sutter and Post. The Plaza's main entrance even opened onto Union Square, and it was closer by a block to the office.

File this case until we get to the Clift. Head down Powell to Union Square and the building that fronts the park on the west:

20 ST. FRANCIS HOTEL

In *The Maltese Falcon* Miles Archer shadows Brigid O'Shaughnessy and Floyd Thursby from the lobby of the *St. Mark Hotel* to his death in Burritt alley. The original of the St. Mark would be either the St. Francis here or the Mark Hopkins on Nob Hill, based on the name and the general description of the hotel as first class. Joe Gores

St. Francis Hotel, 1920s

goes for the St. Francis because the St. Mark is treated in the novel as an obvious landmark, an institution in The City, which the St. Francis was in 1928, having first been opened in 1904 and quickly rebuilt after it was gutted by the fire of 1906. When Hammett was writing the novel, the St. Francis was considered San Francisco's number one hotel, closely followed by the Palace on Market Street. Gores notes that the Mark Hopkins did not open its doors for customers until December, 1926, barely more than a year before Hammett started the book. Even if it is big and is situated on Nob Hill, a year isn't long enough in this burg to become an institution. The Mark Hopkins was no more an institution at one year than the detective practice of Sam Spade would have been: both were just starting out.

If you enter the main doors of the St. Francis on Powell and go into the red-carpeted lobby (in the 1920s a circular registration desk ushered in the guests, but today check-in services are in the St. Francis Tower addition, beyond the original lobby), you're safe enough in imagining you're in the same vast room where Miles Archer was staked out so he could tail Floyd Thursby when he met Brigid here at 8 p.m. When you go back out the doors, you're going out the same way Archer did as he started work on his last case.

The most famous case Hammett claimed to have worked on as a Pinkerton operative in San Francisco originated here in the St. Francis, when the famous Hollywood silent comedian Roscoe "Fatty" Arbuckle had a party Monday, September 5, 1921, in a suite of three rooms — 1219, 1220, and 1221, overlooking the corner of Powell and Geary Streets. After the party Arbuckle was accused of raping the young actress Virginia Rappe; she died September 9th, and Arbuckle found himself on trial for murder in one of the most sensational cases ever to rock Hollywood and America. Hammett said he worked on this case gathering evidence for Arbuckle's lawyers. In the *City* interview both his wife and daughter said they did not think he worked on the case at all, but in another interview in the same issue, an old guy named Phil Haultain claimed that he had worked with Hammett for the Pinkerton National Detective Agency here in 1921, and that both he and Sam Hammett were on the Arbuckle case.

Without question, Hammett was at least in town at the time. His opinion that Arbuckle was framed "by some of the corrupt local newspaper boys" carries that much authority. The image of Arbuckle at over three hundred pounds seems to have stayed with Hammett far into his career, with fat men outweighing thin men in his work, and they outnumber them too. And it is interesting to note that D.A. Bryan in *The Maltese Falcon* clearly is modeled on San Francisco D.A. Brady who went after Arbuckle with everything he had. In a book about the Arbuckle incident, *The Day the Laughter Stopped* (1976), David

Yallop presents good evidence that, to make his case stick, Brady imprisoned witnesses in the home of his assistant district attorneys and forced them to say what he wanted them to say. Arbuckle was going to be his "fall guy," guilty or not, and the publicity would be used to further his career. Reading about the corrupt politics in San Francisco at that time makes it very clear why Sam Spade had to have someone to take the rap for the murders when the falcon proved to be a fake. He would not have the money to get away clean, and the D.A. was already after him as someone he could convict for the killings of Archer and Thursby.

After two hung juries on the question of Arbuckle's guilt, a third jury panel completely acquitted him of any wrongdoing. The scandal, however, ruined his career. He was unofficially blacklisted in Hollywood for some fourteen years and not allowed to act in movies (though his protégé Buster Keaton brought him without credit into his movie *Go West* in 1925 *in drag*, giving Fatty a very funny chance to show the people in Hollywood what he thought of them). Some studios allowed Arbuckle to direct films in this blacklist period, though he could not use his own name — one of the great myths that has grown out of this case has it that Arbuckle directed the movies under the name "Will B. Goode."

Today Arbuckle's name carries the taint of the scandal rather than the vindication of the acquittal, and his films are rarely shown. Before the trial he was the highest paid star in Hollywood, making about three million a year, and only Charlie Chaplin approached him in popularity. He died of a heart attack in the thirties before re-establishing himself with a few short subjects. I have heard both sides many times — he was innocent — he was guilty as hell — but I wasn't there. So I do it like this: the fact that Hammett thought he was innocent doesn't count for much — Hammett also had it that criminals could make jailbreaks while towing along Ferris wheels. I like Buster Keaton a lot, and Keaton thought Arbuckle was innocent — but then Arbuckle was Keaton's mentor and gave him some of his first film work. The opinion that starts to do it for me is this: Stan Laurel and Oliver Hardy thought he was innocent; if Laurel and Hardy think you're innocent, I figure you're probably innocent. But the one that finally does it is that Doug Fairbanks and Mary Pickford thought he was innocent, and the official policy of the Dashiell Hammett Tour is that if Doug and Mary think you're innocent, you're innocent.

Head west on Geary. On the south side of the three hundred block, across from the St. Francis Tower, you might note the Handlery Hotel, formerly the Stewart, where Earl Derr Bigger's sleuth Charlie Chan stops in the beginning of the novel Behind That Curtain *(1928), which takes place completely in San Francisco. The Biggers is a good example of the classical puzzle-style mystery, an entertaining enough read. But if you want a test case to see exactly what Hammett did with the mystery novel in San Francisco and in America, read* Behind that Curtain *from 1928 and follow it immediately with the book Hammett was writing that year,* The Maltese Falcon. *You'll see how thoroughly Hammett blew the competition out of the water for any serious consideration as literature.*

There is another immensely educational comparison you might make: read the Sherlock Holmes story "The Adventure of Charles Augustus Milverton" from 1904, then read the Op story "Fly Paper" (1929). I was attending a meeting of a local Holmes' fan club one night when a woman mentioned that she had by chance just read these two stories back-to-back, and she thought surely Hammett was working his own spin on the same plot Conan Doyle used. No question in my mind about it — what's interesting is to see how Hammett handles the matter of blackmail and compromising photographs versus Doyle's treatment. In Doyle you have the genteel detective tradition in the hands of one of its best practitioners, but in Hammett you have a story as uncompromising as a blackjack, with a gut-punch waiting at the end. No better or shorter education in the classic mystery story versus Hammett will be found.

The next site is at 415 Geary, on the south side of the street, where the banners for the American Conservatory Theater hang in front of the ornate facade of:

21 THE GEARY THEATER

Here the perfumed rogue Joel Cairo, so well-played by Peter Lorre in the Bogart movie of *The Maltese Falcon*, had tickets to see a play. Since Cairo and Spade pause outside this theater in front of a poster of the actor George Arliss in the costume of Shylock, the play must have been *The Merchant of Venice* with its appropriate "pound of flesh" scene (certainly Spade hands more than a pound over to the law at the end of the novel). I don't think it is coincidence that Cairo is a "Levantine," either — Hammett works in the references to Shakespeare adroitly, with my favorite occurring in the next to the last chapter, as Cairo tries to comfort Wilmer Cook, and Wilmer

Geary Theater

smashes him in the mouth. Spade's comment: "The course of true love."

It was a professor, William Godschalk, who pinned down the date of the action in The Maltese Falcon *to five days in December of 1928, using several clues from the novel, paramount among them the fact that Arliss was on stage as Shylock at the Geary Theater at that time.* The Thin Man *likewise occurs in real time — from Christmas Eve 1933 through New Year 1934. Dates for the action in the other novels are probable, though no one has figured them out as yet. They are as time-lost as the statue of the falcon had been until the Greek dealer turned it up again in 1911.*

At the end of this same block on the southeast corner you'll see:

22 THE CLIFT HOTEL

The Clift is Gores' second choice for the fat man's hotel, the Alexandria. It has windows overlooking Geary, but it is by no stretch of reasoning a short walk up Sutter from the Hunter-Dulin Building. I figure one of two situations is occurring here: 1) the easy answer: Hammett did not have specific hotel in mind, hence the contradictions between Geary and Sutter, so forget about it; 2) he *did* intend for a hotel on Sutter such as the Plaza or the Drake to serve as the model for the Alexandria, but when he went to write "the fourth wall . . . was pierced by two windows looking out over *Sutter* Street" he wrote *Geary* by accident and it got into print. Whatever the explanation, a definitive model for the Alexandria is impossible to name.

While looking at the Clift, it's worth recalling that Sir Arthur Conan Doyle, creator of Sherlock Holmes, stopped here the one time he came to San Francisco — from May 30th through June 6th 1923 — at which time Hammett had three stories in print. Doyle was giving public lectures on the subject of spiritualism, which became the major interest of his last years after the sudden death of one of his sons. It is unknown if Hammett went to any of the talks or if his path otherwise crossed Doyle's. At the least, he went into some of the same buildings, because Doyle's lectures were delivered in Dreamland Arena (later the rock venue Winterland, at Post and Steiner), and Hammett opens the Op story "The Whosis Kid" with the Op sitting in the stands at Dreamland, watching the fights.

On the southwest corner of Geary and Taylor stands the:

23 BELLEVUE HOTEL

Fritz Leiber noted that Joel Cairo stays "at the Hotel Belvedere — possibly Hammett's name for the Bellevue." Joe Gores echoes this opinion: "The Belvedere is almost surely the Bellevue." The proximity to the Geary Theater is cited by Gores as support of this hotel being Cairo's. Since he was living in deadly fear early in the novel of encountering "the fat man," it makes sense that he would scurry from his rooms to a theater close by and not risk staying on the streets for long.

Otherwise, no evidence comes out of the book that points to a model for Cairo's hotel — and there is the fact that in Baltimore, the city Hammett grew up in, you'll find the Belvedere Hotel, dating from about 1910. The more years I spend on the streets with the tour, the stronger my doubts become that Hammett had any real hotels in The City in mind for the Alexandria, the Belvedere, the Coronet, and perhaps even for the St. Mark. An arresting stylistic device in *The Maltese Falcon* is that every hotel in which a character stops is given a fake name: no such hotels ever existed in San Francisco. Yet every place where a character *eats* in the novel, when given a name, was an actual restaurant. That point goes against the Belvedere/Bellevue, because the restaurant in this hotel remains unnamed, indicating it was not authentic. Of course, it gets even more confusing. When Sam Spade goes to have lunch in the Palace Hotel (real enough — look down Geary and you'll see it at the foot of the street, across Market), Hammett names the Palace, but that seems to be because it is a place where someone is going to eat, not a hotel where someone is staying. He does not, however, cite which of the several restaurants in the Palace the sleuth may have favored — the Garden Court, or one of the smaller ones.

Perhaps naturally, most people confronted with this problem resolve it by cutting the Gordian Knot in the form of the "Free Meal Theory." But I have profound doubts that a mention in a pulp magazine serialization would have brought Hammett many free meals — and by the time the novel was out in hardcover, Hammett had left The City, only to return for a few short visits. Sure, you may say, to collect on his free meals. No, I think Hammett in this case was having some fun like he did when he created 601 *Eddis* Street — all the hotels will be fake, all the restaurants *real*.

Another point worth note in *The Maltese Falcon* is the presence of homosexual characters. The most discussed aspect of this facet of the novel is the term "gunsel," which many people assumed for years meant a *gunman*, since it was applied to Wilmer Cook. Spade tells Gutman: "Keep that gunsel away from me while you're making up your mind. I'll kill him." Erle Stanley Gardner was the one who pointed out that it was a homosexual term for a kept boy; when Gutman agrees to give Wilmer up for the fall guy at the end of the novel, he is giving up far more than just a hired hand. The sexual overtones surrounding Gutman are amazingly complex — the more credit to Hammett. One aspect of the novel that gets little attention is Gutman's daughter; since John Huston cut her presence from the film version, many people don't remember her even after reading the book. She comes into the action overdosed on drugs, and serves to delay Sam Spade. But one fellow pointed out to me that in all likelihood she is no relative of the fat man — she travels as his "daughter" — but like Wilmer, is along to serve his appetites.

A final thought on this angle: of the five people gathered in Spade's apartment waiting for the black bird to be brought in, three — Cairo, Gutman, Wilmer Cook — are pictured as homosexuals (or, if the daughter is not Gutman's daughter, bisexual). So, you can read Hammett in the 1990s and not worry that he didn't know about what goes on in the world. But I wonder if one of the reasons he brings *these* characters into play in the quest for the falcon is thematic: the falcon originates with the Knights of the Order of St. John — and we've all heard about the sexual proclivities of those monastic crusading orders. . . .

Two blocks west on Geary at Leavenworth, is a place so briefly referenced you cannot determine which building may have housed:

24 FLOYD THURSBY'S APARTMENT

Thursby is one of the great mystery men in mystery fiction. We hear a few things about him: how he was a bodyguard for Chicago gangster Dixie Monahan; how when the States became too hot for him he hopped a freight to the Far East; how he crumbled sheets of newspaper on the floor around his bed at night, so no one could ease up on him as he slept. Yet in *The Maltese Falcon* we never once see Thursby "onstage" — he is always referred to by others, never seen. Even his death, in front of his apartment described only as "Geary near Leavenworth," occurs offstage.

Thursby is Brigid's partner, but a partner she feels she can do without. She goes to Spade and Archer with the story that Thursby has seduced her sister away from their home in the East. She needs to get her sister back from Thursby and returned home before their parents return from a European vacation. (Neither of the detectives believe this story.) Brigid is hoping that Thursby will have a run-in with the sleuth shadowing him and that in the confrontation Thursby will be killed by the detective, or that the detective will be killed and Thursby arrested for his murder. She decides to help matters along by stealing Thursby's gun to frame him for the murder of Miles Archer, but when she learns Thursby has been gunned down in front of his rooms (by Wilmer Cook), she goes back to Spade, knowing she will need help against the fat man.

Now we drop back toward Union Square, then south toward Market, to the next site located on the northwest corner of Ellis and Powell Streets:

25 120 ELLIS

The old Woodstock Rooms, currently the Hotel Pasadena, is where Hammett stayed immediately before he and Josephine Dolan were married on July 7, 1921. The ceremony took place in the old St. Mary's Cathedral at 1115 Van Ness, a cathedral that was razed by fire many years ago.

Directly across Powell from the former Woodstock Rooms, on the northeast corner of this intersection you'll see:

114 Powell

26 114 POWELL

Now the Hotel Union Square, in 1921 it was called the Golden West Hotel, and this is where Josephine Dolan stayed before the marriage. In 1982 this place recognized Hammett's role in its history by opening Dashiell's Bar off the lobby, though Dashiell's closed about 1988. The bartender once told me that soon after it had opened a guy came in saying he was Joe Gores and regaled them with all kind of exotic lore about Hammett. He was an entertaining fellow, the only problem was that he wasn't Joe Gores. They had a copy of *Hammett* at the bar with a photo on the dustjacket: this guy did not write that book. The hotel also opened two deluxe penthouse suites in honor of the connection with Hammett. The "Dashiell Hammett Suite" I understand, another indicator of Hammett's lasting fame. The second one, though, I always had a problem grasping the concept: the "Lillian Hellman Suite." His *wife* is the one who stayed here, not Lillian Hellman.

The final stops for the tour all occur around the next block — easily done by foot, if you want to check your machine into the garage on Ellis between Powell and Stockton. Or you can whip your wheels around the block until you get a good look at these sites.

By foot, move south down the first block of Powell toward the cable car turntable. The Powell Hotel on the west side of this block, incidentally, is where Charles Willeford stayed when he was working on his first novel, The High Priest of California *(1953), a noir episode concerning a used car salesman on Van Ness. Willeford was one of a new generation of writers — Jim Thompson, John D. MacDonald — who started out in the forties and fifties writing "paperback originals," novels that first saw publication in paperback, with covers as lurid as the ones that had graced the pulp magazines. I have three personal favorites in the crime writing arena: Hammett, Raymond Chandler, and Charles Willeford. By the time Willeford began, Hammett was solidly established as first in the field, but Willeford wasn't a writer who ignored challenge. Another of his novels,* Pickup, *also takes place in San Francisco and is a tour de force book-length exploration of the theme Hammett worked in his short story "Nightshade."*

On Market, turn east, proceed past Woolworths to where you will see looming on the sidewalk before 856 Market the:

27 SAMUELS STREET CLOCK

Sometime after quitting his job as an operative with Pinkerton late in 1921 or early 1922, Hammett began to look for a job writing ad copy, either to supplement his income from the pulp fictioneering or possibly with an eye to getting out of the pulp jungle into an easier way of life. He landed a job with the Albert S. Samuels

Company, which at that time was located in 895 Market on the southeast corner at Fifth Street in the old Lincoln Building. Nordstrom occupies the space once filled by the Lincoln — as it faces on Market, it presents much the same height if a far more modern aspect. When you look down the large sheets of plate glass on the ground floor level in Nordstrom, Samuels Jewelers would have occupied the space behind the last pane, right at Fifth. Hammett's presence on this site was acknowledged by Nordstorm and the San Francisco Centre on Thursday April 26, 1990, when a sculpture representing that fabulous falcon from Malta was dedicated in the rotunda.

Samuels Jewelers moved from the original location to 856 Market in 1943, but on March 15, 1990 it closed, and Milens Jewelers does business in the storefront today. The only solid link with Hammett's days in the advertising department ("A Samuels Diamond Will Put You on Top of the World!") is the street clock, a San Francisco landmark. It was installed in front of the original store at Fifth and Market in February 1915 to coincide with the world's fair being held in The City — the Panama-Pacific Exposition, which celebrated the rebuilding of this town after the 1906 fire and also the opening of the Panama Canal. When Samuels moved to this side of the block, the clock came too, and now is the last holdover from that time.

One door west from the street clock you will find the cavernous front entrance to:

28 870 MARKET

The James Flood Building is where Hammett worked in San Francisco for the Pinkerton National Detective Agency under Resident Superintendent Philip Geauque out of suite 314. He was paid $105 a month and was on call twenty-four hours a day, every day. If crime was afoot, the operatives would be at its heels. If not, they would sit idle, waiting for a client to come in and hire them for the next case. From this building Hammett went

James Flood Building in the 1920s

out to fire that housekeeper, to shadow the man whose partner dropped the op with a brick, to interview people on behalf of Fatty Arbuckle's attorneys, to look around Stockton for a jewel thief. . . .

Hammett quit detective work because his health no longer permitted him to continue. He gave a dramatic story about the particular incident that spurred his resignation, of course — and as usual there is doubt about whether or not Hammett personally was involved in this case. His biographer Richard Layman points out that Hammett claimed he worked on the Nicky Arnstein bonds and securities swindle on Wall Street in 1921 — a time when he is firmly placed in San Francisco. In Hollywood, after he came to know Fanny Brice, Ziegfield Follies star and Arnstein's wife in 1921, Hammett told people that he had been assigned to shadow her around New York City a decade earlier, while they kept tabs on Arnstein, and apparently he cautioned everyone he told never to mention it to her.

The particular case Hammett said caused him to throw over his detective career was this: on a run from Sydney, Australia to San Francisco in fall 1921 the Oceanic liner *Sonoma* had $125,000 in gold specie stolen from its strongbox. When the ship docked, the Pinkertons and the local police were all over it instantly, and all but $20,000 was recovered, with the major amount of the haul found in shipboard fire hydrants or strapped to oil cans floating near the liner in San Francisco Bay. The *Sonoma* was readying for the return trip, and Hammett claimed that Geauque assigned him to travel with the ship back to Australia to try to recover the last of the specie en route. They figured the thieves somehow were moving it around ahead of the search parties, and that Hammett might be able to find it by the time the ship reached Hawaii. If not, then he would be on the case all the way across the Pacific. The way he talked about it, Hammett thought this was a great plan — his imagination opened up to the possibility of riding to Australia, getting a job, then sending for his wife and new daughter.

But on December 1, 1921, a last search was made aboard the *Sonoma*. Hammett told Lillian Hellman that he climbed to the top of a smokestack, looked in, saw the gold, yelled that he'd found it — and right then figured he was just too dumb to continue as a detective. If he'd kept quiet until he was out to sea, at least he'd have had an expenses-paid trip to Hawaii and back.

He also said that he found the missing gold under scuppers on a lower boat deck.

In any event, soon after the *Sonoma's* gold was recovered, Hammett resigned from the agency, later in December or in the first few months of 1922.

From casual clues dropped in the first Op novel, *The Big Knockover*, it is apparent that Hammett intended for the Flood building to house his fictitious Continental Detective. It was said to be located in a major Market Street office building some seven blocks from the intersection of Pine and Montgomery, backtracking west along Market from the scene of the big bank robbery that kicks that novel into overdrive. Sure, you could pick another office building — the Phelan, perhaps — but as in the case of Sam Spade's apartment, it seems logical that Hammett would place his detective in the same place he himself worked from, given a clue that brings you so close. The Continental agency is directly modeled on Pinkerton, of course, and the Op's boss, known only as The Old Man, is thought to have been modeled on Philip Geauque.

If the building is open when you do the tour, a walk from the front entrance on Market to the rear entrance in 71 Ellis Street will carry you across marble floors personally gumshoed both by Hammett and by his short fat nameless detective.

Heading from the entrance of the Flood Building to the last stop in John's Grill, you might consider another great mystery of Hammett's life:

THE PUZZLE OF THE JOBS AND THE YEARS

In dealing with Hammett's jobs before his novels threw the limelight his way, I think it is safe to say that he *did* work for the Pinkerton National Detective Agency. It's safe to say that Hammett wrote advertising copy for Samuels Jewelers in San Francisco in the 1920s. Beyond those general statements, you're in trouble. How many years did Hammett work as a Pink? How many years, or was it only months, did he come past the Samuels street clock to 895 Market to write ad copy?

In 1990 the Court of Historical Review in The City chose as topic for its 65th session the question of whether or not Hammett ever worked for Pinkerton. This subject came up because of a 1975 letter to the Hammett enthusiast Hugh Eames, in which W.C. Linn, Pinkerton vice president, indicated that they had no records verifying that the author of *The Maltese Falcon* had ever worked for the agency. During the hearing held in City Hall, Joe Gores testified that he had received a letter from the Pinkerton agency on February 23, 1973, which said that all the records of that era had been destroyed by the agency. In the early 1970s, another Hammett fan named Jack Kaplan, who worked in the West Coast Pinkerton offices, tried to track down case files from the teens and twenties; he said that his researches ended with the information that those records had been destroyed, by accident, in a warehouse fire.

Unless you have some compelling reason to think that Hammett's wife would lie, no good reason exists to doubt that Hammett worked for Pinkerton. Sure, you can say you doubt he was approached to assassinate Frank Little, you doubt the Ferris wheel story, you don't think Hammett sleuthed around for Fatty Arbuckle's lawyers or that he was the one who turned up the missing loot aboard the *Sonoma*. But you'd have to argue with the people who knew Hammett best if you said he did not have a dent in the back of his head or scars on his legs. In her memoirs, Hellman mentions the dent but doesn't know about the brick that caused it — if you like conspiracy theories, I guess Lillian Hellman and Jose Hammett should have gotten the story straight.

The real issues that the Court of Historical Review should have addressed would be *why* doesn't Pinkerton have the records anymore — why were they destroyed — and how long did Hammett work for the agency?

The records wouldn't be a worry at all, but for the fact that Pinkerton preserved the paperwork concerning their pursuit of Jesse and Frank James and the Younger Brothers from the 1800s, which suggests that they have a better grasp on handling case files than their lack of knowledge about Hammett's employ indicated. But even as they were chasing the James Gang, the outlaws were living legends — the great historic interest was obvious. Hammett worked for Pinkerton as a grunt in the teens and twenties; most of his assignments were routine. The reports were not signed by name but by the operatives' code numbers, and were edited by office secretaries before final copy was prepared to give to the client. He did not begin to get really famous until 1930, when the *Falcon* saw hardback print — eight years after he left the agency — and did not become an overwhelming presence on the literary scene until 1934, twelve years after he last worked for Pinkerton. It's doubtful that anyone in the agency would even associate mystery writer Dashiell Hammett with operative Sam Hammett by that time.

The idea that the records of Hammett's era were just tossed out in regular clearing of the warehouse or destroyed in a fire isn't hard to credit. If you like sensation, however, imagine that Pinkerton knew exactly who Hammett was and kept track of his association with the agency and then, about 1951 when he was going to prison for refusing to name names, went through their records and purged all references. I've heard that theory, but if you like that one, try this: it is far more likely that when Pinkerton, Burns, and other major national detective agencies were pulled before Senator Bob La Follette's committee in the 1930s for questioning about their union-busting activities, they went through the incriminating evidence at that point and burned *everything* from the teens and twenties, when strikebreaking was their bread-and-butter.

Hammett's regular claim was that he was employed by the Pinkerton National Detective Agency for eight years.

Richard Layman accepts 1915 as the year Hammett began as an op; this is the date Hammett gave under oath during one of his court appearances in the 1950s. He *may* have started in 1916 or even 1917. He quit in San Francisco in December 1921 or early 1922. You get the figure of eight years if you count from 1915 through 1922, which perhaps is the way Hammett figured it. Of course, he took a year off in World War I, and spent several months after that hospitalized with TB. At most you can credit him with five or six years on active assignment, with maybe as much as eight months of that time working out of the San Francisco office.

The job at Samuels Jewelers is fraught with equal controversy. When William F. Nolan was writing *Dashiell Hammett: A Casebook*, he conducted the only interview concerning Hammett with Albert Samuels Sr., Hammett's boss at the store, who told him that the ex-detective had worked for him about four years. Based upon Veterans's Bureau documents relating to his disability pay, Richard Layman states that "Hammett's full-time employment at Samuels's had lasted about half a year" — some six months in 1926, the period he listed himself in the City Directory as advertising manager for the company. In *Dashiell Hammett: A Life*, Diane Johnson places Hammett, in August, 1927, having lunch with Albert Samuels Sr. and his young son, Albert Jr., in the St. Germaine Cafe opposite John's Grill on Ellis Street (where the Ellis-O'Farrell Garage stands today), and talking business. He was still contributing articles on ad writing to the trade papers by early 1928. At one time I met R. G. McMaster, one of Hammett's co-workers in Samuels Jewelers. Aware of this puzzle, I asked McMaster exactly how long he recalled Hammett working for Samuels. He said that Hammett was at the store for at least a year while he himself was working there, and he was under the impression that Hammett had worked for Samuels at least a year before he began his job.

If we accept McMaster's estimate of two years, along with the known years 1926 and 1927, supplemented by the evidence of the trade magazine articles from late 1926 into early 1928, then 1926-27 are nailed down solid. Of course, it was in July, 1926, that Hammett was found

lying unconscious on the floor of the advertising
department in a pool of his own blood, and later that year
that Samuels gave him the letter that got him his disability
pay. There is no indication in his Veteran's records that
he held a job in San Francisco other than the months in
1926 at Samuels, once he had quit Pinkerton. But
Samuels himself thought he had employed Hammett for
four years.

Samuels Jewelers, 1920s

My feeling is that Hammett did not report his first
period working for the store to the Veterans' Bureau,
enabling him to keep the partial disability payments he
was drawing because of the TB. As soon as he got the

100% disability, the TB was gone — with that money, plus a job on the side writing ad copy, Hammett had enough income to give him the chance to write novel-length fiction. Hammett's loose reporting of his earnings eventually got him in deep trouble with the IRS in the early fifties. He wasn't above this sort of practice, and in the mid-twenties needed all the money he could get, with a wife and two children to support. The hurdle in this scenario is drawing Albert Samuels Sr. into the deal: did he give Hammett a letter saying that Hammett was unable to hold a job and then employ him well into the next year, and maybe the year after that?

Yeah, I think he did. My major reason for thinking so is another story told about Hammett and Albert Samuels: how Samuels made Hammett a loan of some $1000 in 1929 so he could travel to New York and from there make his try at Hollywood. That was the period when the stock market crashed, and $1000 could carry you for a year. A lot of money to extend to a guy who had worked for you for about six months three years before. I can't see it. But for a guy who had worked for you for years, whom you knew and liked well enough to front that letter, I think that's a real possibility.

By 1930 when he had his chauffeur drive him back to The City from Hollywood to repay Samuels the loan, Hammett's spending habits for his movie money were already set: the story is that he gave his former boss back the $1000 in cash, stayed in San Francisco a week buying drinks for everyone he could find, and at the end of the week had to borrow another grand from Samuels to finance his return to Hollywood.

The last stop for this tour will be found in 63 Ellis Street between Powell and Stockton:

29 JOHN'S GRILL

Opened in 1908, of all the restaurants named in *The Maltese Falcon*, John's Grill is the sole survivor of the decades that have passed since Miles Archer cashed in his detective's license in Burritt alley. At 7 p.m. in January 16, 1976, John's Grill officially recognized its part in history by converting the second floor into the Maltese Falcon Dining Room. Around the walls roll still photos and dialogue captions from the Bogart film, and a glass case contains a selection of books by and about Hammett, and even a facsimile of the fabled black bird itself.

The Hammett fan Jack Kaplan was the fellow who talked the owners of the grill into opening a room in honor of its most famous patron. In the mid-seventies Hammett was clearly "in the air" — or in the night-fog. Fritz Leiber in 1973 was doing Hammett research, and he would use Hammett as a character in *Our Lady of Darkness*. Joe Gores was hard at his heels, researching Hammett's life in San Francisco as background for his novel *Hammett*. That anonymous person with the can of spray paint at Bush and Stockton was not the only one who was active.

A third floor Hammett Den was opened Wednesday May 12, 1982, with a Brigid O'Shaughnessy dance floor in the front. If you happen to be in the grill for an event with a live band, request "En Cuba" in honor of Brigid and Sam Spade. This room features photos of Leiber and Gores and William F. Nolan, Hammett and Hellman, and real San Francisco detectives such as Hal Lipset and David Fechheimer.

Disaster struck the night of January 14, 1983, when a fire broke out in the kitchen, causing more than a million dollars in damage. The owners, Gus and Sydna Konstin, rallied and rebuilt, and John's opened again in September 14, 1983, to celebrate its 75th anniversary. Since it is one of the few old-style grills left in The City and the only

John's Grill

place now serving as a Hammett museum anywhere in the country, San Franciscans, mystery fans, and visitors to Sam Spade's burg can only hope it will be around for another seventy-five years.

A couple of coincidental connections (if you believe in coincidence) deserve mention. First, owner Gus Konstin is an immigrant from Greece, and it was a Greek named Charilaos Konstantinides in *The Maltese Falcon* who turned up the black bird after it had been lost to history for seventy years, only to be murdered, the statue stolen. When Gus came to the states he Americanized the spelling of his name, *Konstantinides*, as Konstin. Next, when Gus arrived in San Francisco in 1952, he got his first job in The City as a busboy in Lambo's at 315 Bush Street. Lambo's was owned by Blackjack Jerome, the businessman who gave Hammett *his* first job in San Francisco as a Pinkerton strikebreaker on the docks in 1921. Blackjack Jerome, whom Gus recalls as a real tough guy, died in 1953.

John's offers a souvenir menu featuring an art deco painting of Hammett standing before the grill's door. They serve a special drink, "the Bloody Brigid," which comes in a souvenir glass with a falcon emblazoned on it. And they offer "Sam Spade's Chops": rack of lamb, baked potato, and sliced tomato. In *The Maltese Falcon* Spade drops into John's Grill immediately before going by hired car on the wild goose chase down to 26 Ancho in Burlingame. Spade phones the car company and asks: "Can you let me have a car with a driver who'll keep his mouth shut? . . . Have him pick me up at John's, Ellis Street, as soon as he can make it." Then, "he went to John's Grill, asked the waiter to hurry his order of chops, baked potato, and sliced tomatoes, ate hurriedly, and was smoking a cigarette with his coffee" when the driver came in to tell him he had the car gassed up and ready to roll.

Today, John's Grill is a major attraction for most Hammett fans, the next place to go after a stop into Burritt alley.

•

John's Grill is a good place to rest up, maybe have a drink (Jo Hammett says her father's favorite drink was a double-vodka martini with a twist), and ponder various other puzzles of Hammett's life and writings. For example, did Hammett make up the word "shamus"? Erle Stanley Gardner looked into it at one time, and became convinced that Hammett created the word in a story, just threw it out, and after that other writers, following his lead, picked it up and in time it became part of the language — and eventually the title of a movie starring Burt Reynolds. If Hammett *in 1950* figured that "this hard-boiled stuff is a menace," what if he had lived to see *Shamus*?

My favorite puzzle is one that was brought to my attention by a woman on the tour. For years I had been leading people around, showing them the sites described in this book, places that are real, places that are shadowy and may or may not be based on real buildings, and other places that clearly were invented — 601 *Eddis* Street and its ilk. I tend to be a beer drinker, so I ignore the metaphysical as often as not, but I couldn't ignore it when this woman hit me over the head with it like a brick dropped off the Stockton tunnel.

The puzzle is this: In the literary world Hammett created in *The Maltese Falcon* and his tales of the Continental Op, he was the first writer to give the mystery story the cutting edge of reality. His detectives seldom look for "Truth"; they aren't naive. They work in the real world of facts — of rumors — and of lies. The Op, the most incorruptible figure in Hammett's universe, often uses methods no more noble than those of the criminals he is hunting. The lie and the half-truth are well-polished tools of his trade, though he manages to carve his own sort of morality out of the corrupt society he lives in, and with that and his .38 special, he goes on with his job. Sam Spade is more lured by the temptations offered him than is the nameless short fat detective. If the black bird had been the actual *rara avis* described in Gutman's history of the Maltese falcon, and if Spade could have set up a fall guy for the murders of Archer and Thursby, would he have settled for the spoils, including Brigid, and let murder lie? That possibility lurks over the story like the night-fog. So: Is the metaphysical landscape of Hammett's stories and novels through which his characters travel mirrored in the physical world in which they live and work?

The San Francisco of Spade and the Op is literally built of truths, rumors, and lies: places like John's Grill that are as real as a dime; places such as Spade's apartment and office, described just enough so they may be deduced — with a shadow of doubt hanging on a firm conclusion — and places such as the Alexandria Hotel or Eddis Street which have never appeared on any map of The City. Hammett's detectives move through this city of reality, rumor, and falsehood — a mysterious and dangerous San Francisco created in the pulp magazines of the 1920s that has not lost its fascination nor its hold on our imaginations.

If you want more, you can look up the Pickwick Hotel at Fifth and Mission, the last remnant of the name Pickwick Stage Terminal, where Sam Spade put the black bird in overnight storage. The actual bus terminal was in nearby Jessie Street. Across the way is the Old Mint, which Lon Chaney planned to storm in The Penalty, seven years before Hammett plotted out the heist for The Big Knockover. Less than half a block from the steps of the Mint is Remedial Loan at 932 Mission, the place Spade tells Brigid O'Shaughnessy that will give her the best price for hocking her jewelry, which he insists she does.

Or you might someday hike up Telegraph Hill to Julius Castle on Montgomery, the restaurant where Spade and his secretary Effie Perrine eat lunch in one of the three short stories about the Satan-faced sleuth, "A Man Called Spade." It is impossible to travel more than a few blocks in San Francisco without crossing Hammett's trail.

SOURCES

It would be great if I could write that Dashiell Hammett personally vouched for all the information and theories put forth in this book, but he died before I hit my ninth birthday, so I never had the chance to ask him. With the man himself gone, you fall back on other sources — and then try to figure out which version of "the truth" you like best. Even those people who had an opportunity to talk to Hammett faced the same problem: which version of the story best fits the known facts and the psychology of the people involved? I've presented my arguments already, with most of the information they are based upon gleaned and then collated from the following books and articles:

Anonymous. *Names of Twelve San Francisco Streets Changed to Honor Authors and Artists.* City Lights Books, San Francisco, 1989. A commemorative chapbook issued in connection with City Lights renaming the streets after Hammett, Twain, et al., giving background and details on the project. I'm glad to say that I had almost nothing to do with it, because it took *a lot* of work and even more patience to cut through the bureaucratic red tape involved. I'm lazy and I loathe bureaucrats. I did, however, make one major suggestion to Lawrence Ferlinghetti as he sought out streets with connections to the various writers — I steered him to Monroe Street. At first, he had his eye on Burritt alley. The big problem I saw with that is that Hammett gives Spade's route to the alley exactly in *The Maltese Falcon* and even describes what the street sign looked like at the time. To bring a tour group into *that* alley with the name "Dashiell Hammett Street" would be just too, well, Disneyland-like for me. Burritt is a murder scene, not a tourist trap. So I pushed for Monroe.

Bentley, Christopher. "Murder by Client: A Reworked Theme in Dashiell Hammett." *The Armchair Detective*, vol. 14, no. 1, winter 1981. An article briefly showing how Hammett took the detective-killed-by-his-client-behind-a-billboard theme from the Op story "Who Killed Bob Teal?" for *The Maltese Falcon*. Bentley does not mention the incident with the brick, which seems the most likely setup for the scenario from Hammett's detective days. And it should be noted that he is stating the obvious — and that William F. Nolan in *Dashiell Hammett: A Casebook* and Joe Gores in "A Foggy Night" had made the point already.

Brady, Matthew. "Sam Spade City . . . Just Around the Corner." *Hyatt on the Square*, vol. 3, no. 1, date unknown, but mid-1970s. A short article on Hammett sites within easy walking distance of the Hyatt on the Square, currently the Grand Hyatt, crediting Howard Gossage for his role in placing the plaque in Burritt.

Chandler, Raymond. "The Simple Art of Murder." *The Finger Man*. Avon, NY, 1944. Or more easily found in the recent paperback titled *The Simple Art of Murder*. The best argument ever made in behalf of the hard-boiled detective story as a literary form, by one of the ace practitioners.

Fechheimer, David. "Mrs. Hammett is Alive and Well in L.A." *City of San Francisco*, vol. 19, no. 17, Nov. 4, 1975. The interview with Josephine Dolan and Mary

Jane Hammett. Francis Coppola published *City* during his years in San Francisco, with this issue devoted to Hammett something of announcement for the movie *Hammett,* which was just then getting underway. In addition to the interview with Jose Hammett, this number contains the fragmentary original draft of *The Thin Man*, Gores' "A Foggy Night," and spotlights a painting of Hammett on the cover, among other features. Fechheimer at that time was a partner in the Hal Lipset detective agency (today he has his own agency), and was largely responsible for pulling this issue together. As far as I'm concerned, serious scholarship into Hammett's life did not begin until Fechheimer came on the case. He found Hammett's wife, and interviewed her for the first time, and dug up much of the public documentation (such as the marriage license, finding the marriage had taken place July 7, 1921; since his first daughter was born October 15, 1921, Hammett usually back-dated the marriage to December 27, 1920).

_____. "We Never Sleep" and "I Slept with Man O' War." Also in *City*, Nov. 4, 1975. Interviews Fechheimer conducted with ex-Pinkerton operatives Phil Haultrain and Jack Knight. The motto of the agency was "We Never Sleep"; the always-watching eye Pinkerton used for a logo is thought to have been the inspiration for the term *private eye*, and I wouldn't argue the point. Haultrain presents yet another possible origin for the Maltese falcon: the blackened, jewel-encrusted skull of a Tibetan holy man an uncle sent Hammett from Calcutta, which he figures just *might* have inspired the concept of the bejeweled falcon. Fechheimer mentioned when he addressed the first meeting of the Maltese Falcon Society in 1981 that these ex-Pinks told him that the term operative was not pronounced as operative, but op-er-*ray*-tive.

Geranios, Nick. "Hammett's Sam Spade Might Have Come from Butte Lynching." *The Missoulian*, Oct. 26, 1982. Associated Press wire service article covering Butte bookstore owner Robert Green, and his theory that Hammett may have participated in the lynching of Frank Little. Green takes his theory to the conclusion that guilt over his involvement led Hammett to create Sam Spade, whom Green sees as "highly moral" and incorruptible.

Gores, Joe. "A Foggy Night." *City*, Nov. 4, 1975. The most thorough survey of possible sites from Hammett's San Francisco stories to date, repeating the ones from *The Maltese Falcon* previously located by Fritz Leiber with the addition of several others, plus all the locations Gores could find from the Op series. A cornerstone work.

_____. "Author's Note." *Hammett*. G. P. Putnam's Sons, NY, 1975. Mentions sources used in preparing this novel, many of which turned out to be unreliable. This book must be read strictly as fiction, and not taken as a fund of usable biographical information. For instance, Gores states, regarding Hammett's years in San Francisco, that "the wife who shared some of them is dead." Later in 1975 Fechheimer interviewed her.

_____. "Hammett the Writer." *Xenophile,* no. 38, March-April, 1978. The best short critical statement on Hammett's writing from the point of view of a hard-boiled fan. Gores sees Hammett as "a private detective learning about writing . . . not worried about Literature [but] worried about paying the rent." He singles out Spade's speech to Brigid in which he says "Don't be too sure I'm as crooked as I'm supposed to be. That kind of reputation might be good business — bringing in high-priced jobs and making it easier to deal with the enemy." That professional manhunter's take on *the enemy*, Gores suggests, is the subconscious state of mind "which separates his work from that of Chandler or [Ross] Macdonald or their followers." There are many points in favor of Gores' thesis, but I think it stops short of the area in which Hammett's writing jumps over into the realm of Literature — the psychological effects that adherence to the manhunting code has on his characters. The Op in *Red Harvest* knows he is going "blood simple." The ending of *The Maltese Falcon* partakes of tragedy — hell, it's depressing. (Charles Willeford once told me, as a flat statement of fact, that *all* great literature is depressing.)

Hammett, Dashiell. "Introduction," *The Maltese Falcon*. Modern Library, NY, 1934. Regarding the origins of the novel and the people he modeled his characters on, except for Sam Spade, who "had no original."

Hammett, Richard T. "Mystery Writer Was Enigmatic Throughout Life." *Baltimore News-American*, Aug. 19, 1973. Hammett's nephew gives information on his family history.

Hellman, Lillian. *An Unfinished Woman*. Little, Brown, NY, 1969. Many anecdotes of Hammett from their almost thirty years, off-and-on, together.

_____. "Introduction," *The Big Knockover* by Dashiell Hammett. Random House, NY, 1966. The first memoir by Hellman of Hammett, which presents her picture of his life and work and code of honor, also reprinted as the last chapter of *An Unfinished Woman*. Since then various people have disputed many of the particular points, and Richard Layman prefaces his biography by referring to the "clouded personal image of the man" she had developed since Hammett's death. It is easy to see that Hellman romanticized Hammett, and that clearly is the point to take from her memoir.

_____. *Scoundrel Time*. Little, Brown, NY, 1976. An account of her testimony before the House Committee on Un-American Activities, with information on Hammett's trial and imprisonment and the political atmosphere of the time. (As an example of the kind of error Hellman gets tagged for, on page 48 she has it that Frank Little "was lynched with three other men in what was known as the Everett Massacre"; I've given

the details of Little's lynching and the Everett
Massacre, a separate incident, in the short biography
for this book.)

Huberman, Leo. *The Labor Spy Racket*. Modern Age
Books, Inc., NY, 1937. Based on the Subcommittee of
the Committee on Education and Labor of the United
States Senate hearings conducted in the 1930s by
Senators Bob La Follette and Elbert D. Thomas
(popularly called the La Follette Civil Liberties
Committee), this is the book to go to if you want to find
out what detective work was all about in Hammett's
day. Sure, I've looked into James D. Horan's book *The
Pinkertons: The Detective Dynasty that Made History*
(1967) and others, but this is the one that rang the bells.
Anyone familiar with Hammett's Op and his casework
should find the following exchange from Huberman's
book of interest, as Senator Thomas questions a Mr.
Burnside, assistant superintendent in Pinkerton's
Detroit offices:
     SENATOR THOMAS. How many names have you
     used in your occupation for covering yourself, Mr.
     Burnside?
     MR. BURNSIDE. Oh, I have used a great many
     names, Senator. I have been in the agency a great
     many years and necessarily our work requires using
     an alias a great many times.
     SENATOR THOMAS. Name some of them.
     MR. BURNSIDE. Well I have used the name of
     Bronson and I have used the name of Brunswick —
     oh, a number of them. I generally use a name with
     the same initials as mine, because it makes it easy to
     remember. It is customary in detective practice.

Hunter, Tim. "The Making of Hammett." *New West,* vol.
5, no. 19, Sept. 22, 1980. A feature article on the film
Hammett, with the title-page teaser: "A Coppola
masterwork in progress. Or is it?" This film, which
many people at the time expected to be a terrific
culmination of the new interest in Hammett that started
in the early seventies, bombed. It cost something like

twenty-two million dollars to produce and made about half a million back at the box office.

Johnson, Diane. *Dashiell Hammett: A Life*. Random House, NY, 1983. The biography authorized by Hellman, profits by having access to material held by her, as well as letters provided by Hammett's daughters. I think it is particularly good when it comes to Hammett's last decade, or in dealing with his relationship with his family, but it just slides over the fiction. Unfortunately, in my opinion, no one of the major biographies pulls ahead of the rest as the definitive one to read. They all have good points (this one reprints in full "From the Memoirs of a Private Detective" (1923), and complete letters to Blanche Knopf, etc.), and they all have weaknesses.

Layman, Richard. *Shadow Man: The Life of Dashiell Hammett*. Harcourt, Brace, Jovanovich, NY, 1981. The first of the majors to appear, and the one that packs in the most facts. Both David Fechheimer and William Godschalk abandoned plans they had had for books about Hammett and turned over their research to Layman. This book includes complete transcripts of Hammett's two required appearances over the Civil Rights Congress, and it shows McCarthy's concern over books by Communist writers. I think the drawback to this one is that Layman summarizes all of Hammett's writings and never gets across the idea that Hammett's best work is *fun to read*, which really drags this book down. He agrees with Hammett that "The Gutting of Couffignal" isn't very good, whereas every Hammett fan I know thinks that in this story Hammett was writing at *white heat*.

Leiber, Fritz. "Stalking Sam Spade." *California Living*, Jan. 13, 1974. The cornerstone survey of sites from *The Maltese Falcon*. Befitting its importance, this essay has been in print in the menu at John's Grill since 1976.

Mertz, Stephen. "W. T. Ballard: An Interview." *The Armchair Detective*, vol. 12, no. 1, winter 1979. In this interview, Ballard, who wrote for *Black Mask* and knew several of its other writers, states that at one point — and it would have had to have been the twenties — Hammett "shared an apartment in San Francisco" with Horace McCoy (now famous for his novel *They Shoot Horses, Don't They?* and another *Black Mask* alumnus). Other than this one reference, there is no evidence for Hammett and McCoy sharing a place in The City or elsewhere. The reference books usually put McCoy in Dallas, Texas in the twenties, anyway. I suspect this is another one of those loose statements, like Lillian Hellman's reference to "the girl across the hall on Pine Street," which can't easily be proved or disproved. There is no evidence Hammett ever had a room in Pine Street, either. More, there is no indication that Hammett ever met any other writers in San Francisco. (Although in *Our Lady of Darkness* Leiber pictures a scene in which Hammett encounters the poet George Sterling's protégé Clark Ashton Smith at the midnight burial of some ashes.)

Myers, Laura. "Semi-official: SF 'Judge' Rules Hammett was a Pinkerton Op." The *Santa Rosa Press Democrat*, August 31, 1990. An A.P. wire article re: the Court of Historical Review session which looked into the issue of whether or not Hammett worked for Pinkerton. This write-up notes: "After a 70-minute hearing the judge ruled: 'It is the opinion of this court that Dashiell Hammett did indeed actively work for the Pinkerton Agency on and off for a period of eight years in San Francisco.' " Ooops! Eight *months*, maybe, in The City — eight years, maybe, nationwide.

Nash, Jay Robert. "The Joy of Sax." *Chicago Tribune*, Feb. 28, 1982. Article on jazzman Bud Freeman, with an interview which covers the days in the Aleutian chain when Freeman served with Hammett and thought he was "a super guy."

Nolan, William F. *The Black Mask Boys*. William Morrow, NY, 1985. One of several books that collect stories from *Black Mask*, and a good one to start with. Contains a history of the magazine, and a capsule biography for each of the eight authors featured: Erle Stanley Gardner, Horace McCoy, Carroll John Daly, etc. The Hammett selection is "Bodies Piled Up." (I've had a quibble with Nolan for some time, though, on his praise for Paul Cain's *Fast One* as "the coldest, swiftest, hardest novel of them all." Understand, he's welcome to that opinion. But personally I do not think that *Fast One* would exist in the form it is in today if Hammett had not shown the way with *The Glass Key*, which pioneers that stripped-down style. *Glass Key* appeared in *Black Mask* in 1930, with the hardback in 1931; *Fast One* saw print in the *Mask* in 1932, with the hardback in 1933.)

_____. *Dashiell Hammett: A Casebook*. McNally & Loftin, Santa Barbara, 1969. The first book-length survey of Hammett's life and writing, though flawed as a biography because it appeared before a lot of Hammett's most revealing letters were available, and before Fechheimer did his remarkable research into Hammett's San Francisco years. Joe Gores has praised it for its tone, and it is highly interesting in the sense that the picture it gives of Hammett is the one that hard-boiled fans wanted to believe a decade after his death. This book was awarded an Edgar Allan Poe award by the Mystery Writers of America for best nonfiction of its year.

_____. *Hammett: A Life at the Edge*. Congdon & Weed, NY, 1983. Another of the major biographies. Not as fact-filled as Layman, not as good on Hammett's family life and last years as Johnson, but perhaps a smoother read than either, if you have the inclination to go with only one of the bios. Considering Nolan's long standing interest in Hammett, I had hoped for a hotter book than this one proved to be; still, it recovers much of the material from the *Casebook*, combined with the upgraded info about Hammett's life that had become available.

Petrie, Glynn. "The Looting of the *Sonoma*." *The Californians*, Nov.-Dec. 1985. An article on "the 1921 enigma of the *Sonoma's* stolen treasure," quite detailed. The author does not believe that Hammett could have been involved in the recovery of the gold in the way he said he was.

Samuels, Albert S. Jr. "A. Samuels Tells the Story of the Famous Samuels Street Clock." *San Francisco Examiner*, June 3, 1980. The title says it all.

Stabiner, Karen. "The Greatest Stories Never Told." *New West*, Feb. 1981. An article on nine novels that Hollywood had had in development without success, including *Red Harvest*.

Symons, Julian. *Dashiell Hammett*. Harcourt, Brace, Jovanovich, NY, 1985. In the HBJ "Album Biography" series — lots of photos. A full-length biography, though less than half the weight of those by Layman, Nolan, and Johnson. Symons, an English mystery writer and critic, senses the contradictions in the other books about how long Hammett worked for Samuels, but doesn't go so far as to push his suggestion that Hammett worked for the jeweler for longer than "the best evidence would seem to show." I have a major disagreement with his idea that *The Maltese Falcon's* "effectiveness rests in part in the realization, fuller and richer than in the short stories, of San Francisco's streets and scenes." You want San Francisco, you are much better off going to the Op tales.

Tuska, Jon. *The Detective in Hollywood*. Doubleday, NY, 1978. A survey of detective films, with photos, including long sections on movies made from Hammett properties.

Wolfe, Peter. *Beams Falling: The Art of Dashiell Hammett*. University Popular Press, Bowling Green, 1980. The first purely critical book on Hammett, with the title coming from that part of *The Maltese Falcon* (dropped from the film version by Huston) in which Spade tells Brigid the story about a man named Flitcraft who, when a beam falling from a construction site almost hit him, ran away from his average sort of life only to end up soon after leading almost exactly the same sort of life under another name, in a different town. Wolfe has a chapter called "Sam Spade and Other Romantics," which I've always disliked — Spade is about as romantic as a nail. I suspect that people get confused on this topic because of Bogart, who first played Sam Spade, then went on to play Chandler's romantic detective Philip Marlowe in *The Big Sleep*, and the archromantic figure of Rick ("Richard Blaine, American") in *Casablanca*. One line in particular from this book I like to quote as the single most nonsensical statement about Hammett's work: "Prophetic insight led Hammett to set *The Maltese Falcon* (1930) in what was to become America's most sophisticated city." The fact is that Hammett, living in San Francisco, already had set more than half his stories in the streets he saw every day.

Yallop, David. *The Day the Laughter Stopped*. St. Martin's Press, NY, 1976. A book-length account of the Fatty Arbuckle case, before, during, and after the trials.

•

I believe word-of-mouth has brought me as much information on Hammett and San Francisco as the print sources listed above. Certainly my main impressions of Hammett as a person come from talking with people who knew him.

Doing what I'm doing, people come to you. They phone too. One guy phoned up about three times over a two year period. First time: "Don!" "Yeah?" "Hammett got it wrong!" "What?" "The gun Miles Archer is shot with — it doesn't exist!" "Er . . . okay. Sorry." Second time: "Don . . . uh, I owe you and Hammett a profound apology, that gun, it is a rare type. He had it right." Third time: "Don!" "Yeah, yeah." "In the movie John Huston has the wrong kind of gun!!!" "Yeah, hey, listen — how about calling John Huston and waking him up?"

Someone will have an odd bit of info about a building or a disused street car route — somebody told me once that after Blanco's closed it became Charles' Restaurant, and was vacant for awhile between Charles' and the Great American Music Hall. He said that in the interim period the place was rented by the Mitchell Brothers and used as the shooting set for the notorious trapeze sequence in *Behind the Green Door*.

Some young guys from France came out and kept asking me about all the other novels by all the other guys who wrote for *Black Mask*. I told them that the majority of these other books just weren't available, and they weren't at that time. If you couldn't spring for pricey first editions, you couldn't read most of them. The French hard-boiled fans were amazed, because all of the *Black Mask* writers were in print in paperback in France, and had been for years.

One woman, who had been in one of Hammett's writing classes at the Jefferson School of Social Science, didn't recall any specifics, but retained the impression of Hammett as a wonderful teacher. Another guy had encountered Hammett in Anchorage, when he was about to bail out of the army in WW II; he tried to talk to him about the novels but got only clipped words in response and was left with the impression that Hammett was nothing but a bitter drunk. Another fellow said that he was a big fan of Lillian Hellman, beginning in the late fifties, and that once about 1960 he saw her walking with a very frail old man in Central Park. He went over, said a few words, paid little attention to the companion. In the sixties he started to read Hammett and liked his work even more than Hellman's, and realized that he probably had met Hammett that day walking with Hellman, and had ignored him.

Another man came on the walk who had known Ricardo Cortez, the actor who portrayed Sam Spade in the

1931 film of *The Maltese Falcon*. Cortez's real name was Jacob Kranz. This man said that "Jake" was very excited when he heard about the new version Warners was shooting and desperately wanted to play the part of Spade; because *he* had introduced the character, he felt a proprietary interest in the role. By that time, Cortez's career was well over its peak, and Bogart's was starting to climb, so Jake Kranz didn't have a chance at reprising the role.

The late Richard Ellington, an old line Wobbly, told me about the Frank Little lynching and gave me the title of the I.W.W. history in which I looked up the account of the Everett massacre. His opinion of Robert Green's theory about Hammett's participation in the killing was that it was "interesting in an annoying kind of way. That description could fit several thousand of Butte's residents at that time."

The detail that the Op is reading M. P. Shiel's *The Lord of the Sea* was noticed by Phil De Walt, who told the Shiel devotee John D. Squires, who then told me. When Squires went on the tour, I made a big point of explaining to the others in the group who Shiel was and what he wrote. It would be very hard to locate a more esoteric writer for Hammett to be reading — or calling "a magician" over twenty years later.

Stan Old has been testing me with quizzes from *The Maltese Falcon* for years now. Which cab company did Spade call to get to the Stockton tunnel overpass? Did he go to Burlingame in a cab or a hired car? What was the name of Spade and Brigid's theme song? If I said "huh?" he had the answer ready. Stan is the guy who went poking around in some photo files and came up with the shot of the billboard on Stockton Street that screened Miles Archer's corpse from the casual passerby. Talks with him have honed my perceptions on the *Falcon* more than all the books and articles put together.

Jerome Weidman went on the tour. At the end the fellow who came along with him and his wife nudged him and said, "Tell him you knew Hammett." I recall asking him, "So, how did I do?" and him answering, "Pretty good, I thought."

Brigid O'Shaughnessy's daughter came out — and that's pushing the edge of the envelope even for me. This is to say that the daughter of the woman who worked in the art department at Samuels with Hammett came on the walk. She said that her mother told her that almost every day after work, she and Hammett and the other employees at Samuels would adjourn to John's Grill for drinks. In the *City* interview Jose Hammett mentioned that while he was working at Samuels Hammett "got confused . . . I think he probably started to drink at that time because they were inviting him out here and there." But especially they went to John's Grill.

In 1982 I was on a panel about Hammett's life with Lester Cole, one of the Hollywood Ten.

No doubt but that the Maltese Falcon Society, which I helped found, was a major fund of oral information — David Fechheimer, Diane Johnson, William F. Nolan, Jerome Weidman and many others appeared as speakers. Sitting at the bar, talking with regulars like Mike Keene or Kermit Sheets or Skip Peterson never hurt any. After I met Hammett's daughter Josephine, I asked her to speak; as it turned out, her talk coincided with the fifth anniversary meeting on May 27, 1986, which was also the last — and it could not have ended better. I have included several of her remarks in this book, but I have saved the last question I asked her during the talk for the wrap-up.

People on the tour for years have asked me what exactly Hammett thought about the Bogart version of *The Maltese Falcon*, directed by John Huston. I've never read any remarks, nor do I know of any references in his letters. I asked Jo Hammett if she knew of any opinion pro or con her father had expressed about this movie.

"No," she said, "but what's not to like?"

ABOUT THE AUTHOR

Don Herron has led the Dashiell Hammett Tour in San Francisco since 1977, making it, without close competition, the longest-running literary walk in America. He figures he reached the peak of his fame when the tour turned up on the television quiz show "Jeopardy." Category: American Cities. "The city in which Don Herron leads the Dashiell Hammett Tour." The button is hit. "What is San Francisco?" Of course.

Also by Don Herron: THE LITERARY WORLD OF SAN FRANCISCO & ITS ENVIRONS: A GUIDE-BOOK, City Lights Books. Second edition, 1990.

CITY LIGHTS PUBLICATIONS